THUS FARR

THUS FARR

Tommy Farr

Optomen Press
Published by W H Allen & Co Plc

First published in 1989
by Optomen Press and
W H Allen & Co Plc
Sekforde House
175/9 St John Street
London EC1V 4LL

Set in Plantin by Input Typesetting Ltd, London
Printed and bound in Great Britain by
Biddles Ltd, Guildford and King's Lynn

ISBN 1 85227 017 9

INTRODUCTION

BY
GARY FARR

I was not born until the autumn of 1944, five years after my father had retired from the ring as the undefeated British, European and Empire heavyweight champion.

Later on, when he was to make his brave comeback, I was introduced to the memory I still carry, of my father sitting up in bed, his face terribly swollen and battered.

I remember him as a wonderful father. His wisdom and advice never dictated to me what I must do, only what I should, if I was to be guided by him. Needless to say, when things went awry when I failed to heed him, he was always there to chuckle and help me again.

When I decided, at an early age, that it was a career in contemporary music that I wanted, he encouraged me, saying, 'You know, Gary, that I wanted to be a singer. But in those days there was precious little to be had at that.'

Later on, when I developed pretensions to become a writer, he again encouraged me and told me that he too had written a book. I blush inwardly as I think how I patronized him with his talk of books, but now I remember that it was on his bookshelf that I found *Ulysses* by

James Joyce, *Brave New World, Heaven and Hell* and *The Doors of Perception* by Aldous Huxley. These and many others that I digested at about twelve years old gave me a head start in the world of literature.

When my father was dying, my brother and I left California, where we were living, and travelled to Britain to be with him for one last precious week.

It was one of the most rewarding things I have done. I was able to tell him of my gratitude to him and how much I loved him.

He died with his final dignity and the woman of his life close at his side.

The Christmas after this, my mother came to California to be with her sons and she brought me some papers that she said father had wanted me to have. I had been writing a piece based on his life, so I was hungry for anything else I could use as material. The pages contained in the bulky old manila envelope were largely rubbish, rewritten, sensationalist stuff, churned out by the Fleet Street hacks of the time. There was, however, one page that caught my attention.

An old, dog-eared page it was too, and its heading declared, '*THUS FARR*, by Tommy Farr'. As I read it I felt the hair go up on my head and I got a rash of goosebumps. I feverishly searched for page two, but there was no more. I rushed over to my brother's house, where my mother was staying, and showed her the page and asked her where the rest of it was.

'Oh Gary,' she said. 'It might have been thrown out.'

The outcome of all this was that some six months or so after she returned to England, I received the first of two large bundles out of which I found the original book as written by my father when he was freshly retired from the ring, at the outbreak of the Second World War.

He had been born, on 12 March 1913, in the grimy, poor South Wales coal village of Tonypandy. He started out dirt poor, with little or no education. By the time he came back from America for the last time, in 1939, he was a man of substance, a maths wizard with a literate mind, at ease in the highest company.

It has been a labour of love for me to sort out this book from the thousand pages or so that had languished in his cupboard for so many years. A wonderful exercise in discovering that my father was a man of words. And the evidence of his startling humility, honesty and grace.

I believe that it is a unique work.

No fiction here. This is no invention of the fertile mind. All of which you will read, happened.

May you enjoy it.

Gary Farr
April, 1989

THE BOXING RECORD
OF
TOMMY FARR

1926

Dec	18	Jack Jones	won points	6	Tonypandy

1927

Jan	15	Kid Denham	drew	6	Tonypandy
Mar	12	Dai Davis	no decision	6	Cwmoparc
Apr	2	Alby Davis	lost points	6	Gilfach Goch
Nov	26	S. Hewers	drew	6	Pontypridd
Dec	12	Cliff Smith	won points	6	Cardiff

1928

Jan	21	Evan Lane	lost points	6	Trealaw
Jan	28	Young Hazell	won points	6	Pontypridd
Feb	25	Young Grocutt	drew	6	Bridgend
Apr	9	Young Grocutt	lost points	6	Porthcawl
June	30	Young Howe	no decision	6	Tonypandy
July	4	Evan Lane	lost retired	5	Blaengwynfi
Sept	29	Albert Davis	lost retired	4	Pontypridd

1929

Feb	23	Tom Thomas	won points	6	Ystrad
Mar	23	Len Jones	drew	6	Porthcawl

Apr	27	Kid Spurdle	lost points	6	Porthcawl
May	4	Idris Pugh	drew	10	Mardy
May	8	Herbie Hill	won points	6	Blaengwynfl
May	18	Trevor Herbert	won points	8	Llanelly
June	1	Trevor Herbert	drew	8	Ferndale
June	15	Idrid Pugh	lost points	10	Ferndale
Sept	14	Kid Evans	won points	10	Tonypandy
Sept	28	Eddie Warton	won stopped	5	Porthcawl
Oct	5	Trevor Herbert	drew	6	Porthcawl
Nov	16	Tommy Howley	won points	10	Tonypandy
Dec	21	Billy Jones	won points	10	Tonypandy
Dec	26	Cliff Llewellyn	won points	10	Newport

1930

Jan	18	Billy Pritchard	drew	10	Blaengarw
Jan	25	Llew Haydn	lost points	10	Clydach Vale
Apr	5	Billy Thomas	won ret	4	Penygraig
Apr	12	Emlyn Jones	won points	10	Tonypandy
Apr	19	Walt Saunders	lost points	10	Tonypandy
May	31	Steve Donoghu	won points	10	Tonypandy
June	14	Josh Sullivan	lost ret	7	Llanelly
Dec	27	Herb Moise	won points	10	Penygraig

1931

Feb	2	Jack Powell	won disq	3	Ebbw Vale
Feb	7	Bryn Powell	drew	10	Blackwood
Mar	28	Jack Powell	won points	12	Bargoed

1932

Aug	27	Albert Donovan	lost points	12	Tredegar
Dec	30	Jerry Daley	drew	12	Trealaw
Dec	31	Charlie Bundy	won points	15	Treherbert

1933

Feb	18	Billy Thomas	lost points	15	Bargoed
Mar	25	Bunny Eddington	won points	15	Trealaw

THUS FARR

Apr	21	Jerry Daley	won points	15	Trealaw
May	6	Randy Jones	won ret	6	Merthyr
May	13	Charlie Bundy	won points	15	Treherbert
May	15	Eddie Steele	lost ret	7	Crystal Palace
May	20	Billy Thomas	won points	15	Trealaw
May	22	Tony Arpino	won points	15	Pontypridd
June	3	George Smith	won points	15	Merthyr
June	26	Gunner Bennett	won stopped	5	Cardiff
July	1	Tiger Ellis	won points	15	Tredegar
July	8	Ernie Simmons	won points	15	Merthyr
July	15	Bunny Eddington	won points	15	Ebbw Vale
July	22	Randy Jones	won points	15	Tonypandy

(won Welsh light-heavyweight championship)

July	29	Jack O'Brien	won ret	5	Belfast
Sept	23	Tom Benjamin	won points	15	Trealaw
Sept	30	Charlie Chetwynd	won ret	9	Swansea
Oct	7	Jack Marshall	won stopped	7	Merthyr
Oct	28	Seaman Harvey	won points	15	Trealaw
Nov	4	Steve McCall	won ret	12	Merthyr

1934

Jan	14	Kid Scott	won ko	1	Belfast
Feb	1	Eddie Phillips	lost points	15	Holborn
Mar	26	Jim Winters	won points	15	Cardiff
Apr	23	Jack Casey	lost points	12	Newcastle
May	7	Charlie Belanger	lost points	12	Newcastle
June	13	Eddie Phillips	lost disq	3	Wandsworth
Aug	9	Ernie Simmons	drew	10	Wimbledon
Aug	22	Charlie Belanger	won points	10	Wandsworth
Sept	14	Charlie Bundy	won points	15	Trealaw

(retained Welsh light-heavyweight title)

Sept	19	Dave Carstens	lost points	10	Llanelly
Oct	22	Eddie Pierce	won points	12	Bradford
Dec	21	Pat McCauliffe	won ko	2	Trealaw

1935

Jan	11	Arthur Novell	won ko	1	Trealaw
Feb	4	Eddie Phillips	lost points	15	Mountain Ash

May	8	Manuel Abrew	won ret	6	White City
May	13	Eddie Weinstob	won points	6	Holborn
June	28	Presidio Pavesi	won points	10	Paris
July	20	George Brennan	won points	8	Leicester
Aug	14	Frank Moody	drew	15	Cardiff
Oct	25	George Brennan	won points	10	Leicester
Nov	15	Presidio Pavesi	won ko	4	Paris
Dec	2	Eddie Weinstob	won points	10	Blackfriars
Dec	16	Rhenus de Boer	won points	12	Bristol
Dec	21	Frank Moody	won ko	4	Cardiff

1936

Jan	15	Tommy Loughran	won points	10	Albert Hall
Mar	5	Peter van Goole	won points	12	Swansea
Apr	2	Bob Olin	won points	10	Albert Hall
May	18	Jim Wilde	drew	12	Swansea
Sep	14	Jim Wilde	won ko	7	Swansea
		(won Welsh heavyweight championship)			
Dec	21	Charlie Rutz	won points	12	Earls Court

1937

Feb	8	Joe Zeman	won ko	8	Bristol
Mar	15	Ben Foord	won points	15	Harringay
		(won British & Empire heavyweight title)			
Apr	15	Max Baer	won points	12	Harringay
June	15	Walter Neusel	won ko	3	Harringay
Aug	30	Joe Louis	lost points	15	New York
		(for world heavyweight title)			

1938

Jan	21	James Braddock	lost points	10	New York
Mar	11	Max Baer	lost points	15	New York
July	29	Relinguished British heavyweight championship Deprived of Empire heavyweight title by British Boxing Board of Control			
Dec	16	Lou Nova	lost points	15	New York

THUS FARR

1939

Jan	13	Red Burman	lost points	10	New York
Apr	13	Red Burman	won points	12	Harringay
May	17	Larry Gains	won ret	5	Cardiff
Nov	10	Manuel Abrew	won ko	3	Dublin

1940

Aug	7	Zachy Nicholas	won ret	3	Barnstaple

1941–49 INACTIVE : RETIRED FROM RING

1951

Mar	21	Frank Bell	lost ko	2	Porth
Apr	24	Gerry McDermott	won points	10	Harringay
July	7	Dennis Powell	won stopped	6	Shrewsbury

(regained Welsh heavyweight championship)

Aug	30	Steve McCall	won points	10	Bangor
Oct	4	Robert Eugene	won points	10	Cardiff
Nov	16	Al Hooseman	lost points	10	Manchester
Dec	3	Georges Rogiers	won points	10	Brighton

1952

Mar	17	Georgio Milan	won points	10	Cardiff
May	26	Georges Rogiers	won points	10	Aberbgavenny
July	26	Joe Weiden	won points	10	Worcester
Sept	10	Al Hooseman	won points	10	Cardiff
Nov	2	Werner Wiegand	lost points	10	Dortmund

1953

March	9	Don Cockell	lost stopped	7	Nottingham

AN ESSAY
by
TOMMY FARR

(1950)

A PUG'S PHILOSOPHY

I have fought for my living from an age when most kids would have blubbed if they had been spanked, until an age when I should have known better.

The only sense I may have shown during the thirty-odd years a clenched fist and an open palm were my ways of life, was to become a boxing writer, when the ring could no longer take revenge upon me.

The prize-fighter, for I scorn the class distinction which is sometimes made between the bare-knuckle fighter and the gloved pugilist, is the most vulgarly gazed upon of men. The public allows him no normality of human conduct and there is no escape from the snippety and arbitrary verdicts of scolds and gossips and critics.

So while I give none in return that is worthwhile, I am content at writing around that roped cage where men have fought, some have won, many have lost, a few unhappily have died, and I languished there long enough to know it is the toughest of all sports. Yet I never tried to escape. Why should I?

At the age of twelve I had my first fight and at forty I had my last. At any time I could have quit the ring, but I never did. They threw me in and they threw me out and in all the years between there was never a whimper. It served me well and it served me right.

If you want to know what the conscience of my generation did for me, I will tell you. Do you know how I was educated? . . . in seventeen fights, nine lasting more than ten rounds, for a few shillings, before I was sixteen. Then I went to the University of Joe Gess's boxing-booth and God knows what else besides. My mother dead and my father so stricken that he could not drag himself from his bed to thrash me. Yes, at an early age I took honours in the great humanities. I could recite curses fluently long before I could stumble through the words of *Abide with Me*.

This much I have learned, however. It takes courage to be a pug. It demands the courage of a meaner kind, uncommonly developed, making a man not caring for an ordinary life stand upon his feet to earn with his fists the prize money subscribed by those with no courage of their own. If a pug is a coward he suffers more than a beating. He is scoffed and sneered at and the whispers of 'he's got a yellow streak in him' soon shout in his ear.

Most of the men and women who sit around the ring seem to think of the pug's courage only when they see it ebbing. Then they jeer. They care for nothing but The Punch, The Slam, The Blood and the Fierceness of The Fight. For the countless thousands who mutter, 'I'd get in the ring if they paid me £10,000', there are only a few who ever have the courage to do so. Then the sitters-out make sport of them.

Sometimes it happens that the roar of the crowd brings admiration and hero worship, stirring a whole nation.

These are hollow tributes, floating away like bubbles when the conqueror becomes the vanquished.

Today's champion is tomorrow's has-been. The tide of the ring washes in and it washes up. The flotsam and jetsam are all that is left of brave desperate youths who sail this stormy sea of sport. Did I say sport? Professional boxing is a business, as are so many of the big-time sports. It is a long gamble for the boxer and a meagre moneymaker for all but a few of the men who promote it.

The millions of pounds which, every year and throughout the world, are paid at the box-office, seem to vanish. The ring mysteriously squanders the fortunes it gathers in. It is like a bog. Some men grow corn upon it, but many sink beneath.

The pug knows all this, and the knowledge brings him a pride and wisdom all of it's own. It dawns upon him in those hours of exquisite fitness of the body and self-discipline of the mind which the ring requires. And in those moments he knows, and is entitled to say, that he is more than a pug. He is a man.

His skill and strength, his own driving purpose and zest to win, are his contributions to success.

Opposed to him is the Other Man, thinking, hoping and fearing the same. That is the moment too, when courage takes the place of dread and when self-control abates the wildest instincts. There must be fighting and hurting, but it must be fair and according to rules. That is the only conscience in the sport of boxing, but it is enough.

The contest over, the pug steps down. As he goes, there jostles around him the 'didn't I tell you' camaraderie of go-betweens and twenty-five-percenters. The hangers-on and the brushers-off. They dart like flies around his shoulders. Here and there are those whom he can trust, but they bob up and down, uncertain of their own position in a shadowy world of suspicion.

As a boxer wearily and cautiously stretches aching limbs upon the dressing-room table, the air is saturated with smoke and smell and the small-talk of little men.

Cramp lurks in muscles which have done their task. Bandage and tape are plucked away, releasing, suddenly and painfully, hands swollen by imprisoned endeavour. A turn of the head to catch some smart-alec judgement like, 'Why in Pete's name did you not use that right', brings back the swirl of hurt from near-forgotten blows. The dry tongue runs over the rough ridges of a cut inside the tender mouth, magnifying it a hundred times. There is a sadistic yearning to see in a mirror that bruise on the temple that throbs and throbs. The figures around him blur and distort. At first slowly, then with a rush, comes detailed memory of the fight.

There was that punch in the third round that sank wrist-deep into his middle and drenched him with fear. Perhaps it was trivial after all, for the crisis had passed and the fight went on.

The punch became a commonplace occurrence, but this must have been only because he was winning. He could remember, now, the look of helplessness, the fear of not wanting to be afraid, which crept over the face of his opponent. Soon the fight became one of feet as well as fists. So they were right. Skill and quick thinking too, played their part.

But how those men talked. Why didn't they shut up and go away? Anyone would have thought that they had been doing all the fighting . . . 'I've never seen a better left hand' . . . 'He must have gone crazy to have swapped punches' . . . 'Who's he going to take next?' . . . 'Did you see his kid wife at the ringside? I thought she was going to pass out' . . . 'Those rights to the heart must have half killed him' . . . 'Boy, were you slick to stop that gash under his eye' . . . 'He'll murder that so-and-so next show, if he fights like he did tonight'.

The chorus of know-alls dins out of tune, but then a hand is slapped on his shoulder. His eyelids are raised and a finger that feels like a sword traces the outline of a jagged cut beneath his eye. A man looks at him quizzically, then says charitably, 'He'll be as right as rain after a good night's sleep. Well done.'

It was the doctor. He had gone, leaving behind his reassurance.

So everything was all right. Why not? It was only a fight and it has lasted barely an hour. Go home to sleep. Yes, that's it . . . Sleep and sleep and sleep.

So the boxer plunges on, taking a kindness and a friend wherever he can find them. In the end, after years of this giddy round and when his usefulness is consumed, he slips away to find peace and quiet. He may be richer, or poorer. It is all the same. He has only what he has been able to take and keep away from the others.

He retires with his memories and scars.

Perhaps popularity still comforts him in its lap. Perhaps the forgetful throng blessedly desert him when he no longer wants them nor they he. Yet the itch to fight tantalizes him. Every fighter he sees challenges his conceit. He could still lick them all, he thinks, and his boasting overcomes his discretion. He must return to the ring. This time, however, it will be different. He is experienced now. He knows the game inside and out. He won't be kidded by anything, except, poor sap, by the illusion of age.

He goes only to be swept off his feet by the tyranny he

thought he could defy. Those who cheered his decision now shake their heads. The friends are fewer and the enemies multiplied.

The pug, knowing he is beaten at last, goes home to stay.

All this have I had happen to me. Now, as I write, I am fortyish and ox-shouldered, with a big-headed top to a six-foot frame. I am narrowly but clearly eyed, with a man-made ugliness of nose and ear. I am soft of voice, but still hard of fist. For one glorious hour of triumph but not of victory, fame lifted me upon the shoulders of men.

To those that have you believe that boxing is the 'Devil's Isle of all entertainment', I'd say that I am delighted that I was once an inmate of that island. Furthermore, I'd have you know that I enjoyed every second of my boxing life.

THUS FARR
by
TOMMY FARR

CHAPTER 1

Longer than two years ago I started to write this, the story of my life. It has been hard going, the toughest fight since, unwanted, I happened in a little, overcrowded Tonypandy cottage.

A temptation to quit was often hard upon me when, without the semblance of a guard, I was left to battle not for mere words – they came in torrents – but to catch thoughts and ideas that raced and to dress and drill them as to be understood.

But whenever I despaired of winning what I knew and agreed must be a fight to the finish, I found encouragement, the urge and inspiration to plod on and scratch and scrape- in a common painting of me. That of a man short of thirty, more than six feet tall, big of head, ox-shouldered, curiously nosed, with eyes slit after the pattern of a ferret, an ear thickened, a bowelless fellow quick to anger, just and only a pug, impossibly rough, uncouth, the stormy-petrel of the ring.

Then with teeth snapped shut, jaw squared, I would leave my corner, so to say, left hand straight, the right dynamited, and hammer out a different from an accepted picture of Tommy Farr.

I write with my soul laid bare.

I am no angel. There are no angels in Tonypandy nor yet in all the coalfields of my native Wales.

I was born in poverty and, like the rest of a considerable brood – there were eight of us – reared on a hardness that was as iron.

My father, a Cork Irishman, was a miner with a passion and a relish for knuckle-fighting, in which, since it was the law of the mountains, there was no softness in him. He allowed none in others.

Not until my mother, no older than thirty-two, died.

Then the steel in him rusted and cracked.

Counted by years he was young, but under the weight of the loss of his lovely Sarah Owen he wilted and crumpled as will a tree blasted by lightning. And then there came a day when he was stricken by paralysis, and toddler though I was I helped in a general tugging of him into the motherless home. For the rest of his days that spread over years, long interminable, cruel years they were, he lived on, hopelessly crippled, speech stolen from him.

Kindly neighbours and folk from around and about shared our grief and woe, and there was preaching and praying loud and long.

Realist, if not heathen, that I was, I could not understand, and I was rebuked for the devil that was in me.

I refused to believe that 'it has to be'.

How so? to the horror of 'my betters' did I pipe and scream my disbelief.

'Tommy Farr,' it was sing-songed, 'it is wicked that you are.'

I remained a rebel, dry eyed and consumed with bitterness, beyond weeping and wailing. Only did I feel pain and puzzlement and tragedy and my own futility. For what could a boy that I was, or indeed my brothers or sisters, do?

Pride, empty bellies, guts found a way. We banded together, the big and little of us. Overnight the girls changed into women, boys became men with heads high and challenging.

Anything and everything we did.

We sold reels of cotton and cheap haberdashery from door to door and, in season, home-brewed herb beer to earn desperately needed money.

But in my conceit and certainty that I could do a full-grown man's work, I decided that that was not enough, and while I itched and ached and hungered for the 'big opportunity', I prayed that my dumb, paralysed father might be released from a living death, as I knew that he himself prayed.

Yet I was afraid that he would be taken away. He was my father and to appease a terribly smitten conscience I would, in my dreams, unlock his prison and free him of his manacles to see him as I first remembered him, a giant of a man, assured of a long and full life. Stern, unbending, ruthless, the maker of his own laws, preaching and practising the gospel of the big stick.

As I studied him during the five years he lived on uncomplainingly, heroically, I was taught an unforgettable lesson in fortitude.

'Tommy,' his eyes spoke, 'take all that's coming to you, and it will be plenty, and you will pull through. They'll knock you down, but you will get up and fight on as I shall fight to the last gasp.' And under the stare of a shell of a physically magnificent man of but yesterday, it seemed, I swore by all the gods that I was prepared for the worst.

A battalion of savage was born within me and from the mountain-tops I roared defiance, the louder when, with my brothers and sisters, relations, friends unknown and unsuspected, I followed my father to his last resting place. My Celtic fires raged and blazed in a riot of imagination. I tingled with a physical bigness that was my very own, convinced by the roughness and readiness of upbringing that the road to victory was through the strength of endurance.

Always at my elbow was a skeleton of leanness, and deep down inside me a sense of frustration. So it was that I determined that with half a chance I would break away from the slavery of being at the beck and call of anybody and everybody for the odd shilling.

In my early teens, not an hour later than schooling (of which I had little or none) permitted, I was working in the coal pits of the neighbourhood with Jack Stock as my 'butty' – a ganger or foreman, you would perhaps call him. Jack Stock and philanthropy were strangers. 'So much for me, what's left over for you' – that was our agreement, which he himself framed according to general practice.

He saw to it that I gave all that was in my half-naked, sweating, ceaselessly toiling self. There was no complaint or rift until, with a weekend hangover upon him, he lashed out at me with a shovel and cursed me for being lazy.

I sacked myself on the spot, cashed in my pay ticket to become a Jack-of-all-trades: in turn kitchen help, a waiter of sorts, furniture remover, fireman on a Thames garbage boat, anything that was going. There were long nightmares of unemployment when it was as if all doors were closed to me. I was poorly clad, ill fed, biffed and out, and in railings against bad luck I gave rein to a temper quick to rise.

Yet in my worst tantrums I clung to a sureness of a brighter, better tomorrow.

Much store I put on what not a few of my critics have been pleased to call Welsh craft and cunning. And if craft and cunning are cardinal sins, I have committed them. I ask for no forgiveness. I am what I am – a fender for myself. For so was I born and taught and made strong in a belief that anything worth while must be fought for. It is the religion of the coalfields. I have tried to live to it, and have so far succeeded that rated by everyday standards I am considered to be more than passably rich. So long as I remember my beginnings and ride bridled to the end of the road, I may never know poverty and the awfulness of its grind.

'Lucky Tommy Farr.' How familiar the chorus. It is nearer to the truth to say that by persistency, dog instinct, cussedness if you will, I have escaped from the wolves of which the prize-ring abounds.

To those without knowledge and experience of the underground of professional boxing, the whittling down of a fighter's earnings is a science beyond comprehension. Whales and minnows alike are the feeding ground of the parasites. In no well-ordered state would they be tolerated; they are as blatant as they are rapacious and unscrupulous.

Boxers who battle into big money, if they are to enjoy the lion's share, must of necessity be armour-plated to hold up under the guns of the leeches, feather-pluckers, ponces and chisellers. There is no market so black as the fight market, no body of men more shamelessly exploited than the professional pugilists whether champions, near-champions or novices.

By and large the trade of fighting is in the hands of the racketeers. Square-dealers there are, of course, but they are pathetically few and far between.

I solemnly declare that if I had not been taught as soon as I was capable of understanding that it was up to me to decide whether I should sink or swim, I would have finished where I began. With nothing.

Then there came into my boy life a truly remarkable man, Job Churchill, who having had a leg torn away while working in the pits, had set himself up as a saddler. A rarer, richer character there could not be. No scholar, yet full of learning, a textbook on matters and things that go to the root of life, stark and real.

I saw then, as I do today in all my grownupishness, a guiding star. No commitment have I made without first seeking his advice. None would I enter into without his approval.

Job Churchill took the place of my father when, having kicked in as a coal miner, I would go and unload my troubles in his busy workshop.

'Tommy Farr,' he said, 'I'm not blaming you for chucking the bloody pit. For what's the difference between murder below and murder above ground? If you must be killed, be killed in broad daylight. The black devils of the pit pulled the leg off me. They might have sent me to hell mangled, as perhaps they meant to do. There's not much for the likes of us, anyhow, my son, only what we fetch and hold on to.

'There are more bare than full cupboards in 'Pandy. Look around – more youngsters out of work than you can count. If you hang on here, the dole will rob you of whatever your spirit. It will freeze you up. You've got to fight.

You were born and meant to fight. Leave 'Pandy and its shrivelled pap.'

A strange surging happiness told me I had found a sheet-anchor in this man of flesh and blood and ready understanding. He did not prate as did the Bible thumpers. His language was the language of the pits, easy of comprehension. His sadler's shop became at once my classroom, playground and clearing house of my trials and tribulations.

I hankered after a trade. There was none that I could learn and, besides, I could not afford the luxury of an apprenticeship. I loathed the pits, but the more I groped for salvation, the more the snags. I was in danger of becoming an out-and-out rebel, when Joby found a way out.

'They tell me,' he said, 'that you've been boxing,' and nailed me with his gimlet eye. 'You might do a damned sight worse than making a scrapper of yourself. That, I know, would be to risk being broken into little pieces. But you are an outsize in kids and if you'll let me screw your head on the right way, you'll be none the worse for the clouting.

'I don't say that you'll strike the road to a fortune if you make a whole time job of scrapping, but have a shot at it and I'll watch your step.'

With Joby's blessing I offered myself to Joe Gess as a fighter at his booth at Tylerstown. I was then rising sixteen. Joe gave me a once-over and decided I was too little to join his troupe. 'But,' he said, 'you can clock on as a handyman.'

Good enough: I was at least sure of my keep though I knew that for every bite I would have to pull my full weight and that no sooner a word than a blow.

Nothing goes 'by your leave' in a boxing-booth. There

are no niceties, none expected. But in Gess's booth I found humanity.

I often wonder whether the crowd, as they are invited to 'have glove', have a thought for the men paraded outside the booth to take on all comers. Whether they regard them as a race apart, whether they credit them with having feelings, whether they believe they have a soul above the trip-hammer, whether they only see in them the derelicts of the ring or, at best, to be life's Aunt Sally to be shot at and toppled over by the lusty Toms, Dicks and Harrys of the fairground.

In Gess's booth I found and lived with 'white' men, true soldiers of fortune. There is small, if any, place for scallywags in a well ordered boxing-booth.

I was proud when I was voted big enough and good enough to take a place in Gess's troupe of fighters. As a means to learn the trade of fighting it is beyond price. To every fight-minded youngster I strongly recommend the boxing-booth as the best teacher of all. An unholy grind it is to be sure. A cracking, crunching, smashing thing. But it does teach all that is demanded of a pugilist – the will to win no matter the opposition or the odds.

After nearly two years in the booth I took on a notion that I was ready to crash into the fight game proper. Job Churchill was of that way of thinking too, but with this warning: 'You'll have a long way to travel before you touch the big money even if you clear all the decks in Wales. If you pay your way and have something left over as you go along, you'll need to thank your lucky stars.'

Joby, as usual, was right, for although I quickly made a local reputation, big purses were not for me. Even when judged by the records that I had got to the top of my native tree, I had to be satisfied with what I could cop.

TOMMY FARR IN AMERICA

A Copy of the Poster Announcing the Forthcoming Fight for the
HEAVYWEIGHT CHAMPIONSHIP OF THE WORLD

WORLD'S INTERNATIONAL HEAVYWEIGHT CHAMPIONSHIP

YANKEE STADIUM

157th ST. & RIVER AVE., N. Y. CITY

Auspices of 20th Century Sporting Club Inc. and Free Milk Fund for Babies Inc. - Mike Jacobs, Promoter

THURS. AUG. 26
8.00 P.M.

15 ROUNDS

JOE LOUIS
WORLD'S HEAVYWEIGHT CHAMPION vs.

TOMMY FARR
BRITISH EMPIRE HEAVYWEIGHT CHAMPION

TOMMY FARR

OTHER STAR HEAVYWEIGHT BOUTS

ADMISSION $2.50 · RESERVED $3.50 · $5.75 · $11.50 · $16.50 · $23.00

INCLUDING TAX

Tickets on sale at N. Y. Hippodrome, 6th Ave., 43rd to 44th Sts. Phone MUrray Hill 2-6901 and at Yankee Stadium, Phone MElrose 5-0900

MAYOR CITY JOB PRINT INC. 166–168 WEST STREET LONG ISLAND CITY, N. Y.

NOW READ THE

NEWS OF THE WORLD

for TOMMY FARR'S OWN STORY (Exclusive Cables)

Tommy Farr in America

Tommy Farr (left) with his old friend Job Churchill walking in Tonypandy a month before Farr's fight against Burman at Harringay on 13 April 1939.

Associated Press

Tommy Farr (Wales) went on to beat Clarence 'Red' Burman (USA) on points over 12 rounds.

Topical Press Agency

Tommy Farr, the British heavyweight champion, having defeated Walter Neusel, a week previous, paid a visit to Aberdare on 17 June, 1937. He was already a folk hero.

Fox Photos

oxing provided a way out for Tommy Farr. He walked to London from Tonypandy
the Great Depression looking for work. Few would be so enterprising today.
ventually, it paid off. Here, Farr arrives back from America on the "Queen Mary",
th amongst others, his sister Sally (right).

Keystone (11 October, 1937)

Left: Max Schmeling, the German heavyweight, and Tommy Farr, the British and Empire heavyweight champion, sign a contract on 22 June 1937 to fight at the White City Stadium on a date yet to be fixed.

Left to right: Schmeling; Brig-Gen A.C. Critchley and Farr in Brig-Gen Critchley's office in Pall Mall.

Graphic Photos

Thomas George Farr in the RAF in the 1940's. He wanted to serve his country so badly that he was devastated when he was told that he would not be able to do this on active service.

ADAM HATS, by jove!
They're Tops!

Tommy Farr

British Heavyweight

Fame had its price …

Above: with George Formby, July 1940.
Columbia Records

Above right: advertising Adam Hats.

Right: Madame Tussaud's
Fox Photos

There was an occasion when I expected at least £50 when I called for my 'end' for a ten-rounder billed as the second attraction of a show at Cardiff. The promoter, without batting an eyelid, grumped, 'There's nothing for you young feller-me-lad. You were on a percentage of the gate. There ain't no percentage, the weather killed the show. You're unlucky.'

'But,' I reminded him, 'what about training expenses and what not?'

'Look here, Farr,' he snorted, 'I'm not in this for the good of my health. After paying the guaranteed purses, there's nothing left. So what?'

'This', I hissed, as I banged my fist on his office table.

'Here's a tenner then,' he relented.

'Make it fifteen and we'll cry quits,' I rasped.

Whether he saw red in my eyes I do not know, but he sprung an extra fiver.

Sequel: After my fight with Joe Louis he came up in London's Mayfair hotel, all fuss and froth, to offer his congratulations.

'Let me see . . .' I asked. 'Aren't you the "fighter's friend" and "jolly old sportsman"? The fellow who gave me the air when I asked to be paid for the fight I had for you? It's not such a long time ago that you can have forgotten. Take a walk with yourself all the way back to Cardiff, and may you find it still raining.'

'But . . .' he excused.

'Get,' I snarled. He got, and in the liveliness of a long memory, I attacked my dinner with gusto.

Provocative, truculent Tommy Farr, you might decide. But that would be as mother's milk to what a London cartoonist broadcast in New York a few days before my fight with Joe Louis.

'What chance,' he was asked, 'has Farr of beating Louis?'

'About as much as Shirley Temple.'

I heard him giggle into the mike as I sat, all tense in my training camp at Long Branch. He got a laugh, no doubt. But to me, he was not funny. With all the mellowness that has come to me, I have not forgiven him.

And I shall never forget his sacrifice of cheap wisecracking at the expense of his fellow countryman on the eve of the battle of his life. My immediate reaction was to storm. I jumped away from a game of poker in which I had found distraction and locked myself in my bedroom where, scalded with indignation, I tossed and turned the night long.

I can hear the voice now: 'If Tommy Farr has a chance of beating Joe Louis, so has Shirley Temple.'

The sting of it, however, has given way to supreme thankfulness that I have not only survived the 'knockers', but need not fear, whatever the rains, in the days to come. That is an enormous something. Infinitely more than I had dared to hope for even in my wildest dreams and fancies.

During the first two years after I quit the boxing-booth, the going was terribly hard.

In a fight with Tiger Ellis, the Welsh welter champion, I had to retire in the fifth round with a slit eye into which an inflammation set. I was kept on the shelf for months, and although when fit again I twice beat Jerry Daly, the native middleweight title holder, first for a fiver a side over fifteen two-minute rounds and again later, over fifteen threes for a tenner a side, there was next to nothing in my locker.

I was eighteen, growing fast. What I could put away in eats was nobody's business. Half starved and with nothing in or around Tonypandy that I could do outside of the pits that I loathed, I walked to London, where I arrived with a few shillings at the most.

Regular lodgings were out of the question. I became possessed by such a sense of loneliness that if it had been physically possible, I would have trudged back home. I found harbour with a night-watchman, who having shared his supper, allowed me to sleep in his hut on the Embankment.

I hunted days-long for a job and was about to give up the ghost altogether when the good watchman, handing out a chunk of bread and a rasher of bacon, inquired, 'Any luck, son? Don't tell me. I know. I hears they want a fellow to stoke up on that rubbish barge that goes from here and up and down to Shell Point. It ain't no picnic. But if you can put up with the stinks, and it don't 'arf hum, it's yours for the asking.'

I was on that barge like a fly on a horse-cloth.

Smells, evil and persistent, were nothing compared to what I went through in that stoke-hole. I stood five feet ten inches, after allowing for a slight stoop not uncommon to swift-sprouting youngsters. The hole did not allow by inches for a fellow so tall, and there was nothing for it but to do the shovelling from an almost kneeling position.

For some months I carried on at thirty shillings a week. Stripped to the waist, I suffered torments of hell under the dripping of condensed water from the hot pipes that splashed on my bare back to raise balloons of blisters. And at nights, when rugged up in the scuppers, sleep was worse than a mockery. I squirmed and sweated myself into a bag of bones until, wracked with pain, I threw in my hand.

Another soul-destroying prowl for any kind of job.

Only casual work came my way, and that terribly ill paid.

With the little I had saved I managed, with a tightened belt and by counting every penny, to afford lodgings in the neighbourhood of Edgware Road. But the Wales I had sworn not to return to until I had made good, was forever calling, and I panicked with homesickness.

The problem was how to get back to Tonypandy, short of tramping.

I was reduced to a last half-a-crown, when I was invited by my fellow lodgers to join in a game of solo. I fell, but the angels were over me. I won consistently and readily agreed to higher stakes.

Three pence, sixpence, a shilling. My luck held.

With hearts as trumps my opposite neighbour went 'abundance on spades'. 'Abundance trumps,' I shouted, white about the gills. Romping home, I grabbed the kitty and, deaf to curses, I found that all told I was more than £7 to the good. I had skinned the school.

The following afternoon I was at Paddington Station bound for Wales. Before I could line up at the booking office, I bumped into a 'Pandy man.

'It's Tommy, indeed it is,' he spluttered. 'If you're going home it's not the fare you'll have to pay for,' and he slipped the return half of his own ticket into my hand, explaining, 'It's not going back to Cardiff that I am.'

I was first in the train that went back to South Wales, where I arrived in the late evening. From Cardiff, the walk to 'Pandy was a mere doddle. Fourteen or fifteen miles.

It was about two o'clock in the morning when I reached home. Out popped the sleepy head of my brother in answer to the rattle of the pebbles I threw at the bedroom window.

'It's you Tommy, is it,' he sung in Welsh. And in a tick he was down and had his arms around me.

In the light of the kitchen lamp, we stared at each other,

half choked with the lump that was shot into our throats. Then, all for my ravenous, hungry self, a quart of cockles, a loaf of bread and a pot of tea, brimming over.

I stoked an empty, rumbling belly to the full.

If I live to be as old as Methuselah, I shall never forget that meal.

CHAPTER 2

That meal galvanized me into life.

I lied to my brother as I told him how well I had done in London. My pinched face and the clothes that hung loose about my lean frame and the half shut eyes that begged for real and long sleep, told him that I had lied. In the late afternoon, which was as soon as I had awakened, I promised myself that never again would I run away.

Only to Joby Churchill, whom I looked up at the earliest opportunity, did I tell the truth. He listened in silence with the knowingness of an owl. When he found speech, this is what he said.

'It's not sorry for yourself you should be, but thankful. You have learned the first and most important lesson of all. A lesson in realism. You were born in the gutters. The only hand to help boy or man is his own. You have been made sore, but in soreness there is knowledge to be found that is in no written book. Joby's been doing a lot of thinking since you stole away, and though God forbid that I put false notions into your young head, I believe, that after what you've gone through, you might do worse than try to make a living with your fists.'

24

'Joby,' I broke in, 'I've got to be a fighter or nothing. Get me the fights and the rest is easy.'

'Not as easy as that,' he cautioned. 'I cannot be your manager even if I wanted to be, which I don't. The most I can do is help in launching and steering the boat. We'll get caught in many a squall before we reach dry land, and perhaps strike the rocks.'

It was slow to take definite shape, but the ups outnumbered the downs, though after paying expenses there was no more than a small margin left. In between fights, Joby fed me with books on travel, and with a fired imagination I saw in him a Don Quixote come to life, myself as Sancho Panza, as did Dan Parker, the famous American columnist, when we happened in New York.

To Parker, who excelled as a lampoonist, Joby was as manna from heaven, ready-made articles by the score. For many parts did Parker cast Joby. 'The Mountain Sage' . . . 'The guy who does his sleeping standing up' . . . 'The sucker who isn't' . . . 'The wooden-legged oracle'. Of American experiences and all that befell me in the States I will tell later.

So back to my apprentice days, during which I confined my activities almost entirely within a radius of twenty-five miles. To most fights, I travelled with an ever-increasing army of rooters, by charabanc, singing as we rolled along through the valleys, with Joby leader of the choir.

Great fun and spice it was, even on journeys when I had been licked. For we took new heart in the certainty that there was another day when experience and physical odds would not be so heavy against me and the rough edges in my make-up would have been smoothed away.

In return matches, one after the other I accounted for the few opponents that beat me, and thanks to the shrewd gambling of Joby Churchill and the sternest thrift I saved enough money to buy for my family the cottage in which I was born.

And how proud I was, to be sure.

The little house was a wonderful mansion. Farr's Castle, remote from meanness and leanness. So I bubbled.

But having covered and re-covered the local fight circuit, I was seized by restlessness. The cure for which, Joby decided, was a 'damned good hiding'.

I confessed then that I had received an offer of a fight with Eddie Steele, whom many considered a likely heavy-weight champion of the near future, at Crystal Palace, and it had given me an itch to try my luck in London. 'Well,' allowed Joby, 'I suppose there's nothing for it but to take your hook.' I did. And this is what happened.

I took the ring wearing a gum shield for the first time, terribly conscious of greenness. All went well until the seventh round, which came with me holding what I reckoned to a winning lead.

From the start, however, I had been fearful of swallowing the shield, a cheap, ill-fitting thing. I stopped for a second to adjust it. In that second Steele swung his right to my chin and knocked the contraption down my throat.

Instead of trying to cough it up, I jumped over the ropes, raced blue in the face to the dressing-room, where under the weight of a thump on the back, the shield flew out. Off I went at the double to climb back into the ring, only to find that the fight had been given to Steele, as was proper.

With the bottom of my world fallen in, I sought comfort in Joby.

All he offered was a reminder that I was 'a blasted young fool'.

'How do you expect to win,' he asked, 'with that contraption stuck in your chops? It's garrotted yourself that you did.'

It was a tailless Tommy Farr that arrived back in 'Pandy.

But I so reacted to the scorn of Joby that five days later I was on the warpath again. At Trealaw I beat Billy Thomas. Within a fortnight, at Merthyr, I was well in front of George Smith at the end of fifteen rounds. And on a first appearance at Cardiff, I knocked out Gunner Bennett in the fifth round.

Ten consecutive victories followed, including one over Randy Jones for the Welsh light-heavyweight title. The following week I was fighting Jack O'Brien in Belfast and won by a knockout in the fourth round to begin a happy and profitable association with Ireland under the direction of Jim Rice, a great sportsman. Seven bouts running I won against, in turn, Tom Benjamin, Charlie Chetwynd, Jack Marshal, Seaman Harvey, Steve McCall, Leo Evans and Kid Scott.

Again London called. This time it was Eddie Phillips and again I was the loser over fifteen rounds, but only on the post, at Holborn Stadium.

I was not satisfied and my dissatisfaction became the more acute when some four months later we met at Wandsworth and I was disqualified for what the referee decided was a foul at a moment when I was in a fair way of taking the full measure of Eddie.

But there, it was set on record that I had burned a third London boat. I was spared the doldrums by the simple and only philosophy of the ring: 'It's all in the game'.

Says I to myself, 'Tommy, bury yesterday. It's stone dead anyway. You may not capture London, but it's not the will-o'-the-wisp you believe it to be. It can and must be caught.' Impatiently I waited for my next job, and then the best I could do was to draw with Ernie Simmons at Wimbledon in London's suburbs, which performance, however, won praise of the critics.

I was back at Wandsworth within three weeks and beat the much travelled neck-or-nothing Charlie Balanger, the French Canadian, but after beating Charlie Bundy for the Welsh light heavyweight championship, I slipped up against Dave Carstens, the South African.

Fights with Seaman Harvey, Eddie Pierce, Pat McCaulife and Arthur Novell, each of which I won. And then, early in 1935, came what I voted was the chance of a lifetime . . . a fight with Eddie Phillips for the British cruiser championship at Mountain Ash.

In preparation for it, I pitched camp at the Swan Hotel, Penygraig, Tonypandy, to apply myself for the first time to special training, replete with real live sparring partners. I was somebody at last, a regular card. But, ten days before the fight, I broke a small bone in my right hand, 'and that,' I cried, 'has torn it.'

'Perhaps,' comforted Joby, 'you can poke Eddie's head off with your left. It's no use asking you to call the fight off. If you do, you'll get nothing and you'll have to pay the expenses of training. What does a man do when he finds himself between the devil and the deep blue sea? Why, he takes a chance. And that is what you've got to do. Meantime, mum's the word and prayers for the best.'

'That's OK by me,' I agreed. The idea of letting £150 escape me and having to dig into my hard-earned savings for expenses was unthinkable.

In a burning eagerness to 'touch' for my share of the purse, I neglected to keep an eye on the scales, and when two days before I was due in the ring I weighed at a local coalyard, I found to my dismay that I exceeded the cruiser limit by six and a half pounds.

'That,' moaned Joby, 'is worse than having only one hand.'

The verdict of an inquest we held on the spot was to check up on the scales at the chemist's shop. They showed that I was six pounds too heavy.

A starvation diet and violent physicking was prescribed, together with rubbing and the nearest thing to plain roasting and boiling.

On the morning of the fight I went to Dan Jones, the fruiterer. His scales told me I was one and a half pounds overweight.

More physick and ripsnorting massage. After which, in fear and trembling I went for the official weigh-in. It was found that I was a couple of ounces under the limit, and somehow I disguised that I was as weak as a cat. Back at my quarters I drank quarts of milk, put a chicken out of sight, and after a rest I found that there was little or no tiredness in legs that a few hours before had threatened to buckle up.

I went the full fifteen rounds and although my right hand was useless there was no more than daylight between us at the finish. Although I say it who perhaps shouldn't, Phillips only scraped home. In that I was frightfully handicapped physically, I had good reason to be satisfied. I was £150 to the good, instead of being out of pocket, but when I came to think things over, I realized to my sorrow that I stood no higher than 'just a Welsh champion' and that merely a local reputation cuts no ice.

There was only one thing for it, I decided, and that was to set up and operate from London. I was tired and weary of being classed a small-town fighter. 'It's not worth it,' I convinced myself. And so I moved to Slough near London where I settled with the rest of the family in a house which I bought.

About this time I put myself under the management of Ted Broadribb. No throwing-over Joby Churchill. Never: he remained and still is my counsellor-in-chief. For nearly four months after my fight with Phillips at Mountain Ash nothing came my way except Manuel Abrew, the coloured Scottish heavyweight, whom I met and stopped in the sixth round at the White City.

If I were asked to date the beginning of a successful attack on London, I should say it was on a May night of 1935 when I fought Eddie Weinstob 'the Alberta Cowboy', then something of a vogue. Weinstob was a tough, tearaway youngster. His pilot was Kaplanski, who banked on Eddie making a clear sweep of the decks before taking him to New York. Our affair, which was the feature of a tournament organized for the Greater London Fund for the Blind, was limited to six rounds. Odds were laid that Weinstob would knock me out. I won comfortably on points.

Weinstob, who told me that he had agreed to fight me for a handful of dollars, took the defeat so much to heart that he did little good afterwards.

'I guess,' he confessed, 'I didn't know what a bum boxer I was. It's me for the home ranch.' Nice boy, Eddie.

Jeff Dickson did not have to ask me twice to appear at his Palais de Sport in Paris the following June – first because I had not been to France and, most important, I was keen to make good in an international sense. Dickson put me up against a Presido Pavesi. I was the winner over ten rounds. Off to Leicester for George Brennan, who as an amateur had proved too much for the rest of the cruisers. I beat him in that and in a later fight.

Doubling back to Paris I knocked out Pavesi in four rounds, got the better of Rhenus de Boer at Bristol, knocked out Frank Moody in four rounds at Cardiff and started to prepare to meet Tommy Loughran, the undefeated world cruiser champion who had won high favour by giving a boxing lesson to Maurice Strickland at Wembley. As a reward for defeating the especially tough New Zealander he hoped to get, if he was not actually promised, fights that would bring him more money than he was likely to get in the States.

Some of my American friends will perhaps have it that Loughran had had his big days when he was here, but those who saw him will agree that rather than being at the end of his fighting tether, he held to heaps of style and cleverness, and that he still ranked as a master boxer. A knockout specialist he was not; he was an artist. In Philadelphia, his home town, he was a darling of the gods. During the twenty years or so he was in the ring he fought in all the cities and towns of America, making and holding to contacts that brought him vast knowledge, if not an immense fortune.

There was much that was pleasantly different from his contemporaries in Tommy Loughran: he was the other, the human, side of the picture of the American pugilist after popular conception. He talked as well as he could box. He made many and lasting friendships here. And pleased I was to fight him.

We met at the Albert Hall under the direction of Jeff Dickson, a month after he had beaten Andre Lenglet, a French heavyweight of whom there were high expectations in Paris.

The betting was on Loughran and through Joby Churchill I helped myself generously to the odds. I was returned

31

the winner on points, and according to my reckoning, justly so. Loughran, however, was sure that he did enough to deserve the verdict, but like the old campaigner that he was, pocketed whatever his feelings and ideas.

I am not giving to jump to conclusions, but after beating Loughran I was confident that a claim I made to a fight with Jack Petersen for the British heavyweight title would be conceded almost as a matter of course. Even as a commercial proposition I expected that promoters would go to any lengths to bring us together.

I was conceited enough to suppose that of all the challengers to the title I had done as much if not more to prove that I approached nearest to the champion. I was quickly disillusioned. Not only did Petersen give me the cold shoulder, but the Board of Control passed me by, nominating instead Len Harvey upon whom Petersen had turned the tables at White City, and as if to rub it in, they set up Jock McAvoy as second best of the country's heavyweights, 'which,' Joby Churchill in his choicest Welsh decided, 'beats cockfighting.'

For myself, I am afraid I said things more pointed than discreet. I was left to freeze. I remained in the ice-box for nearly two months.

Then the Dutch caveman Peter van Goole arrived in Swansea, where I fought and beat him. As a boxer van Goole was no high flier, but I give my word that you might hit him with everything short of the bucket and he would ask for more. The harder he was hit the greater his capacity for absorbing punishment. Knocked down, he would bounce up.

It did not vitally matter, apparently, whether he was cut to ribbons, cracked plumb on the jaw or had a ramrod of a right sunk in his belly. Wire-haired, worse-for-wear-faced van Goole remained on the premises.

If ever a man gave all he had for little more than a bare living, it was him. It is only in the ring that such men happen. Why he was not carried away more dead than alive from Swansea is beyond me to explain. I hit him with everything during the twelve rounds over which the fight was spread but he was still roaring defiance at a limit to human endurance at the finish. Even did he manage to conjure a smile as he took himself off for repairs.

About this time Paul Damski, who had for his trumpcards Walter Neusel and Eric Seelig, brought to London Bob Olin who a few months before had lost the world's cruiser title to John Henry Lewis.

I went after Olin at racing speed. Jeff Dickson made haste to make a match which was put on at the Albert Hall within three weeks of my affair with van Goole. I needed little special training and Olin for his part declared that he wanted only light work to get into tip-top condition. Further, he made no bones that he had the beating of me. Such was his confidence that he might have been out for a holiday when he toed the mark. He was so cocksure, as was Damski too, that Joby Churchill, getting the office from me, got busy amongst the betting boys, who were offering a shade of odds on the American.

I won on points over ten rounds. I forget what my end of the purse was. It was certainly not a fortune, but with the harvest from the betting, I was content.

Olin was like a man in a bad dream when he realized that he had lost, and was not lifted out of it when he turned to see Damski collecting towels and sponges and what-not, throwing daggers of looks. Olin did not fight again in this country. There was no market for him. Returning to New

York he was knocked out by John Henry Lewis in an attempt to win back world honours. A little longer than a year after his fight with me, he closed down at the end of a short and none too profitable tour of Australia.

Having disposed first of Loughran and then Olin, I again pressed for a title fight with Petersen, but whether the gallant Jack had no stomach for me or whether the underground wire-pullers meant to keep me out in the cold, I could only guess. The fact was that the louder I clamoured for a match with Jack, the higher went their noses in the air. I was experienced enough in the ways of the black market to allow that there was no logic in the affairs of the ring, but for the life of me I could not square the attitude of the Board of Control with common justice. I asked for nothing more than favourable consideration of a claim based on achievement. That, so it seemed, was too much.

I was brought to earth by Joby Churchill.

'Tommy,' he advised, 'take a grab at yourself and hold on. The moon and the stars are for no man and that's what you'll find yourself crying for if you wet-nurse grievances. To hell with the jobbers and such-like. Leave London. Come back to Wales and sure as fate they'll be running after you.'

I left my home in Slough and went to live with Joby.

I found training irksome and took on so much fat that I was in a fair way to pass as an alderman when, a month after getting back to 'Pandy, I fought Jim Wilde at Swansea. I only drew with big Jim and in belief and hope that London's big-shots would perhaps look more kindly upon me if I met and beat him decisively over the championship distance for the Welsh heavyweight crown, I immediately begged for a return match. It took Wilde four months to accept my challenge, and for a second time we fought at his native Swansea. During the interval I could get no worthwhile fight, try as I would. However, having got into shape I knocked Wilde out in the eighth round and returned in haste to London, only to find in another hunt after Petersen that when he next fought his opponent would be George Cook.

At the end of three months the best that Broadribb could find for me was Charlie Rutz, the credited best of the French heavies. A match between us was put on at Earls Court four days after Petersen had out-pointed 'Grand Old Man' Cook.

In a long lay-off I had put on so much weight that when I got on the scales for Rutz I was sixteen and a half stone and wheezing like a grampus. I had been given the wire that Rutz would be easy and that I would doddle home; that at the most he would not last longer than four rounds.

The noble Charles, far from being easy, was not only as strong as a bull but gored and roared like one. At the end of the first round Joby Churchill, who as usual was in my corner, dinned into my singing ears, 'Tommy, if they are not putting it across you, I'm a Dutchman. It's a ramp.' I sweated with suspicion that ate into me, and cursed for not having taken the Frenchman seriously. I groaned and grunted under the load of a couple of stones or more overweight. Before half the distance had been covered I was dog-tired and as slow as a shirehorse. Those who have seen Rutz must have marked his physical hugeness. He saw to it that in the clinches I carried every ounce of his bulk.

To cut a sorry and to me hair-raising story short, I scrambled, but only by sheer will power, to the end of the twelfth round, which was the last, and I was the winner. Joby was in such a stew that I had the greatest difficulty in getting him to see that if he did not give me a hand I would flop in my corner. I might have been hamstrung for all the use in my legs. However, with his help I managed to duck between the ropes and get to my dressing-room. There I fainted and was out to the world for goodness knows how long. When I came to, it was to the swearing of Joby. It was merciful that those around did not understand a word he said as he let off his Welsh steam.

All I got for the fight with Rutz was £20. As a bear with a sore head I returned to 'Pandy, there with Joby to do some hard thinking.

CHAPTER 3

News had been making the rounds that the promoter
Sydney Hulls, who had left Wembley to join forces with
Harringay Arena, was in America and was bringing the
brothers Max and Buddy Baer over, the idea being that
Max should fight Petersen.

'That looks as if I am to be snuffed out altogether,' I
feared.

Joby came out of a brown study to do a fandango.

'Listen,' he piped. 'I'm not seeing green elephants. It's
only that it's a hunch that I've got. It is this: there's coming
soon the biggest boon ever and if we mind our Ps and Qs
we'll strike lucky. Doll up and let's go see Petersen have
his third fight with Neusel. They tell me that Jack is pretty
certain to wipe out his two defeats by the Boche. Suppose
he doesn't. What then? Why, there'll be nobody to fight
Ben Foord for the title. Nobody except Tommy Farr.

'As I see it, Hulls is counting on Jack to upset Neusel's
apple cart. That would leave him with the choice of
Petersen or Foord for Max Baer. If I know anything, it is
that Foord will be in no hurry to fight Max. It is short
odds that if Neusel again stops Petersen, Jack will retire.

So what? With Baer in his saddle Hulls will be so much up a gum tree that he will come to us and we will say, "Give us Foord", with a definite understanding that if we take the title from Ben we've got first crack at Baer.

'Meantime we've got to sit tight. No more scrounging around for jobs with cap in hand. From now on, we are the gaffers.'

Joby in his Sunday best, myself decked out, up we went to Harringay to join a crowd that filled the stadium to overflowing.

There was not a rooter that rooted harder or louder for Petersen than myself. My Welsh blood boiled over, and to the singing of *Land of My Fathers* I gave the fullness of my leather lungs. I fought for Wales, for Jack Petersen. I was with him in the striking of every blow. I *felt* every blow. It was as surely my affair as it was my countryman's.

By comparison Jack was as a ballet dancer is to a clod-hopper, a fencer to a blacksmith, a splendidly trained athlete to a lumberjack. That is how I figured as Jack tip-toed into the attack and with a left hand as straight as a die sent back the square head of the German with a jolt and brought stars into his blue eyes. It seemed that Neusel could no more have stopped a left hand than he could have jumped the moon. So much was immediately obvious.

'Joby,' I sung to Churchill, 'Jack has only to box him and he'll cakewalk it.'

But Jack could not see that which was as plain as a pike-staff. Instead of darting in and out and pinking and poking and stabbing, he took to rushing and tearing. Worse for him, he made no allowance for the roughness of the German in the clinches, with the inevitable result that he spent strength needlessly.

'For the love of Christ, box him Jack,' I yelled.

'Tommy,' nudged Joby, 'Petersen is beating himself. Watch. There he goes with no defence to even a blind swipe, getting close instead of shooting from a distance. If he's not squeezed to death by the blasted Prussian Bear, he'll be half blinded by a swinger.'

This is what happened. The eyes of Petersen to which in his recklessness he gave no protection, were badly damaged. True to race and breed Neusel revelled in punishing a crippled opponent. He might and could and should have knocked out a Petersen robbed of all of his magnificent spirit: he preferred the way of the inquisitor. There was a bully in Neusel as there is in many Germans.

It is neither prejudice nor hate that makes me say that there was a moment in the early stages of that fight, when had it not been for the curses and threats of Damski from his corner, Neusel would have quitted. As I took stock of him, I was convinced that in the make-up of Neusel there was a yellow streak. If Petersen had done no more than obey the alphabet of boxing he would have won easing up. But . . . Well, you know Petersen, his qualities and shortcomings. Gallant, indeed, but how he wrung out tears of blood when in this last of three battles with Walter Neusel he sacrificed himself on the altar of his own impetuosity.

'Joby,' I broke a painful silence as we left Harringay, 'I'd give both ears for a crack at Neusel.'

A few days later we were off to Bristol, where I knocked out Joe Zeman in the eighth round. Then back to 'Pandy where we anxiously waited developments.

With Petersen out of the scheme of things, Sydney Hulls did not have to ask me twice whether in the next Harringay promotion I would fight Foord for the championship. I could not sign up quick enough, and off I went to train at

White Rock, Penygraig, where I got into grand shape. Nevertheless I had a strange feeling that after the long wait for recognition I would slip up. It seemed too good to be true that I was to fight for the British championship.

When I got into the ring I so steeled myself against dangers as to see trouble where there was none. As round followed round, some devilish imp inside me muttered, 'One false step and back you go to a desert of despair to be laughed and mocked at, and you'll finish where you began.' I could see myself back in the pit, again on the tramp to London, in the stoke-hole of the Thames rubbish barge . . . All the miseries and privations of my youth did I feel, until Joby, sensing and feeling the mental tortures I was suffering, whispered as I returned to my corner after the third round, 'Did you hear them shouting for blood? To hell with them. If they want fighting hot and strong, let them do the fighting. You box, try nothing you are not sure you can do, and you'll win by more points than you can count.'

I knew Joby was right. So it was to murmurings of impatience for gore that I attempted no more than I could manage. I was content to so tie up Foord that he not only dropped points but could not break through the defence I built. In that way I became the British heavyweight champion.

Critics without exception declared that it was an especially dreary business, that no title fight could have been so barren of thrills. One of the newspaper boys, who shall be nameless, declared it to be lousy. 'Tommy Farr, a real champion? Never.' He read into my showing an unpardonable affront, to himself in particular, for which there was no forgiveness.

I freely and frankly confess that my fight with Foord was

not up to the standard by which a championship is judged, but was I wholly to blame for leaving the crowd cold? If I were a cheap champion, what about Foord? Why didn't he knock me for six? For surely since I was no better than a small-town fighter, it should have been easy for the man who sent Jack Petersen crashing to defeat. In the belittlement of myself an injustice was done to Foord: he was no chump.

I do not seek to excuse what I agree was a colourless display, but I might have been spared some of the basting.

I fought Foord according to plan, the plan of a man who knew that if he lost he would be thrown on the scrap heap. I did not expect bouquets. I did not get one. I doubt whether I was given so much as a handclap. Perhaps it was as well that I was given the frozen mitt. Otherwise, being human, I might have reached for and worn an outsize in hats.

Joby Churchill advised an immediate return to Tonypandy. 'For listen Tommy,' he begged, 'if we stay in London we'll be pestered to death and we'll not be able to see the wood for the trees. It doesn't matter a curse whether you please the critics and pull faces at the sensation mongers. You are the champ and don't forget that Sydney Hulls has got to find someone for Max Baer. We're on velvet. No more grubbing along.'

As cat and mouse we settled in 'Pandy. Word came that Sydney Hulls had been given plainly to understand that there was no chance of the Board of Control allowing Baer and Neusel to fight: it was against the rules for two foreigners to engage in a match. Max Baer had been so hotted up and he himself had so caught London full in the eye, that something had to be done.

If there is a better showman than Max I do not know

him. But he is not only priceless entertainment: he is 100 per cent sportsman. We have hammered hell out of each other, but he's my good friend as I know that I am his. There is no pettiness in Max, neither in Buddy. Max may want a deal of understanding, but once you strip him of cap and bells you'll find none of the clown. Nowadays he is a serious sober family man and although he has been a hard spender, I should say that he is comfortably off. It was his good fortune to be looked after by Ancil Hoffman, a kindly-spoken man who knows the fight game from A to Z and whose word is his bond.

I make no apology for confessing that when Baer came here I got him wrong. Perhaps it is because he was so enormously different from other fighters, native or foreign, I had known. That by the way.

While Baer was being shown around, Churchill and I were at 'Pandy with our ears to the ground waiting for the first sound of the approach of Sydney Hulls. Telephone calls we did not answer, telegrams inviting me to London we did not open.

'If there are to be any conferences they must be held here,' declared Joby. 'This is where we put the screw on. They've got to use Baer and whether they like it or not they've got to get you to fight him else send him back and cut their losses. It isn't your ugly mug they want: they want Tommy Farr, the British Champion, and they have got to pay your price.

'It's not for them to say we'll give you so-much: it is for you to *name* how much. And Tommy, there is no taste in philanthropy, not least in the fight game. For the first time we're the governors.'

With that fixed hard in my mind, I went to London and didn't I drive the best bargain for myself. To General

Critchley, Colonel Wilson and Sydney Hulls I was a nut that couldn't be cracked except upon terms. I got what I wanted for signing up, and I give you my word that it was more than I received for all my other fights up to that time put together. Precisely the amount is my own affair. Only will I put it on record that Harringay treated me handsomely.

And guess my reaction to the sudden and stupendous change of fortune? I so stitched up my pockets that neither myself or anybody else could dip into them. I counted every copper before spending. Maybe in padlocking my purse I earned, if I did not deserve, the sharpest criticism. I was no Gaspard, however. Brought up as I had been by the scruff of the neck, having from my earliest days known want, I was determined that once I got among the big money I would get the fullest value from every shilling. I was under no delusions. 'Once you lose your sense of values,' I assured myself, 'you'll find yourself heading for the gutter.'

So it was that I practised thrift to such a degree that when I look back I am neither surprised nor pained that I was twitted for close-fistedness. The contrary: I am thankful that I did not buy popularity, which, rightly or wrongly, I felt was denied me.

It was agreed that my fight with Baer should be put on a month after my win over Foord. The choice of training quarters was much debated. To ensure generous publicity which it was felt that I needed, it was suggested that I should prepare in London. I was all for licking myself into shape in Wales, but eventually I compromised by setting up camp in the outer London suburb of Blackheath, having first taken soundings that I could be sure to enjoy quiet. I was thoroughly at home at Blackheath. The country atmosphere suited me down to the ground, the food was good and wholesome, there was no fuss, no ceremony. There was no lack of sparring partners and, better still, I was free to do my work in a gymnasium that was never over-crowded. I thrived on my preparation: there was not a single rift, no cause for worry at all. We were one happy family.

Before the end of the first week at Blackheath I sent for Joby Churchill. I said, 'They tell me they are betting any odds on Max, as much as ten to one. I hope what I hear is true. In any case you go and back me for any amount. Take £500 to start with. I'm game to gamble up to a thousand. Bet like blazes. I couldn't be fitter and don't forget that Baer has had a long lay-off, whereas I have been fighting all the time. How do you feel about it, Joby?'

'Tommy,' he answered, 'what they say is all my eye and Betty Martin about offering ten to one on Baer. He's favourite all right, but not at ten to one. This is going to be a fight, and you can take it there'll be no such odds. If we sing low we might get fives. At a showdown, say three to one. But leave it to me, I'm going into the market with the gloves off, to bet like stink.'

Joby was as good as his word. He bet right up to our limit and with such shrewdness that when we came to strike an average, the odds he got worked out at roughly four to one; and he placed bets in such a way that the 'boys' had only the foggiest idea that we were the biggest operators.

In my scrapbooks I cannot find a single prophet who did not plump for Baer. I am well within the mark when I say that few fighters have been greater outsiders than myself. All the thunder was for Max. I was rated a little higher than a useful Dobbin, which remembering the showing of

Foord and myself in the championship was not surprising. Every day during my preparation at Blackheath I read of the wonderful things Max was doing in his camp, down Kingston way. That never was he fitter. Only praise for Max. I was not considered worthy of a single headline.

The fact was that my training had little colour and I had no stories to tell. Frankly, by comparison with Max I was no sort of publicity.

A week or so before the fight I was asked to make an appearance at a tournament down in Brighton for the Harry Preston Memorial Fund. The occasion, I decided, called for a new suit and I squandered fifty shillings for plus-fours. So decked out I was terribly sure of myself. With Tom Evans, my trainer, I travelled by third class ticket to Brighton where in my self-importance I expected to be received in a manner befitting the newly crowned British champion. There was not so much as a hand-shake for me, and off I trudged with Evans to the Hippodrome where I found that Max and Buddy Baer had already arrived in state. They had travelled from London in a gorgeous cara-van pulled by a Rolls-Royce and had been given seats of honour at a banquet. Max was the only one to give me a really glad hand.

I stood first on one leg and then the other waiting for my turn in a belief that I was not wanted. I was about to double back to London, when I found myself being led by the hand on to the stage to be introduced to a packed house as the man who was to fight the great Max Baer – 'Tommy Farr, the British and Empire heavyweight champion'. I was cheered to the echo. Never sweeter music than the bellows of welcome that greeted me. My spirits rose from zero to sky high. I did my piece and with a new heart hurried away to catch the last train to London and on to Blackheath.

All went smoothly in what training there was left for me to do. I cannot explain it, but it is the gospel truth that the nearer the night of the fight, the greater my confidence that I would win. Twenty-four hours before I was due in the ring I took Joby Churchill by the ear and gave him £100 to back me at any odds he could get at the ringside. That, I insisted, was my own personal bet.

'If that's the way you feel, Tommy,' said Joby, 'then I'm going to help myself too.'

I have often been asked what I felt like when I left my dressing-room and came into the arena to a fanfare and with the spotlight full upon me. I was seized with a strange coldness. Not a coldness that comes from apprehension. I had no fears. I was certain that only an accident could deny me victory. But it was a coldness that blotted out the crowd and deafened my ears to clamour. I felt terribly alone until all the lights in the stadium were set dazzling and Baer, having acknowledged a thunderous welcome, walked to my corner with 'Hello, Tommy. Guess you're feeling pretty good.'

'Never better,' I replied and ducking my head between the ropes I called to Tom Evans, so that the laughing, playful, wisecracking Max could hear, 'Tom, this is going to my night of nights.' And to Joby, who was plucking at a towel, 'Don't forget the bets.'

'Good God, go easy, Tommy,' was the answer of the overwrought Joby. A pretence of listening to the referee's instructions was ended by Max giving me a hearty pat on the shoulders and back to our corners we went to wait for the bell.

Max came to me stretched to the last inch of his considerable height. I crouched and weaved into the attack and at once planted a light left on his nose and, dodging a vicious right which he sent by way of reply, I two-fisted his ribs. Max grinned as if to say, 'There's no weak spot there, Tommy.'

'You can't kid me, Max,' I said to myself. 'The fighter with a foolproof belly doesn't live.'

My central purpose, however, was to prod him as often as I could with the left hand and if possible goad him into letting go all he had. As I scored to get into a definite lead I could hear Ancil Hoffman, his manager, urging him to go in and make a fight of it. Max sniggered his certainty that I would quickly tire and then he would open out. I did not tire in the least although Max, in the clinches, not only made me feel his enormous strength but the viciousness of the bite in his short arm punches when we were at close quarters. My training however, had left me without a physical flaw and what mattered most was that I enjoyed complete mental serenity.

Whenever Max stood off and stuck out his left hand, sure enough he would let go his right for a knockout, only to find that I had either stepped clear or was beating a left-handed tattoo. Let there be no misunderstanding. I had many anxious, if not definitely bad moments, for when Max gets the full weight of his punches home, something oftener than not either bends or breaks.

Fortunately for me he failed to break down my defence and I beat him for speed. Also, I had a surer sense of distance, but a twelve-rounder, as the fight was scheduled, is a long way to travel and well did I realize that no matter how far Baer was behind on points as likely as not he would, given the least rope, win with one punch. Outside my corner and the singing Welshmen squeezed together on the topmost tiers, lookers-on had no doubt about Baer winning. Max certainly encouraged such a notion by his indifference to the rat-a-tats of my left hand and to the frequency with which I made him miss.

When he did brace himself for the 'kill', I punched and cut his eye. From that moment I was certain that I could only lose by a fluke.

His best round was towards the end, when he caught me with his right and dug his left into my stomach. Buddy Baer shouted, 'That's it, fight him, Max. You've got him, sure.' The effect Bud's cry had on me was to challenge Max to stand toe-to-toe. He accepted, to the cries from my corner of, 'Get away, Tommy.' I gave a deal more than I received, however.

By then the damaged eye of Max was closing fast. In the clinches he puffed and blew and although before the final bell he forced out of himself all he had, the referee found at the finish that I had won well.

If I had not done a little dance I would have busted for joy. Speech was burgled from Joby Churchill: he could but let cry and stump around to the singing and whooping of my countrymen.

Max, with his eye now tight shut, came over to me to say, 'Well done, Tommy. I guess you licked me fair and square.' And believe me, he meant every word he said.

As soon as I could tear away from well-wishers, I made for my dressing-room to find it crowded with back-slappers. You know the kind, the fellows who go with the wind and tide and don't mean a thing. I dressed anyhow, and professing weariness by way of dodging invitations to feast in the West End, made tracks for Blackheath with the faithful Joby and Tom Evans. My sisters were waiting for me with kettle boiling and tea ready to be brewed. Out of the oven were brought fish and chips on which we banqueted. And having feasted, we sang and laughed until long past midnight, rounding off the celebration with games of cards.

It was near to four o'clock in the morning when we broke up, from which hour I slept like a log until past noon, when Joby, after a scratch meal, took charge. Said he, 'No more hanky-panky, Tommy. We're going back to Wales by the first train. If there is any more gadding about, you and me are going to fall out. It's got to be 'Pandy and more hard thinking. The tide's at the flood, and if we stay on here we'll miss it. You've picked up a heap of money. There's only one safe place to put it – the bank. If you don't save it, the wolves will be after it. I've been doing some reckoning and I should say that, all told, you've raked in the better part of £5000. That's not the earth.

'There's a sight more coming your way if you don't get off the rails. You've turned all the laughs in your favour by plugging and plodding and slaving. Keep at it, give the gushers and the mouthers a wide berth. "What I have I hold" – there's your slogan.'

We returned to 'Pandy. Don't laugh: when I squared accounts I had to thump myself into believing that so much money was mine. I argued with Joby about the need for swell clothes, a motor car and odds and ends that would be in keeping with a changed and exalted position.

'Tommy,' he just barked, 'don't be bloody daft.'

So I had to be content to lord it in my fifty shilling plus-fours and a 'Sunday best'.

Meantime Max Baer so capitalized his personality that he remained the biggest card in the Harringay hand. He offered no excuse for his defeat; he left that to the critics, who as a body I had yet to win over. I was not peeved on that account, but I was most certainly at a loss to know what I must do to get definitely into the news.

Through Sydney Hulls, Harringay suggested that if I came to London I might steal some of the limelight. But I was under a pledge to Joby Churchill to lay low. 'The only way to send your stock up,' he insisted, 'is winning, not by showing off at parties and guzzles. Your gym is the place for you and is your shop window.'

Under all the pressure I could screw up, Joby allowed a couple of days off for me to look up Frank Godfrey at the Star and Garter, Windsor, where Walter Neusel was marking time, hoping, I suspected, that the Board of Control would relent to the special circumstances and lift the ban on fights between two foreigners. I was having a meal at the Star and Garter with a friend when Neusel came up and so far as it is possible for a German to be funny, he played the part of humorist for all he was worth; and I joined in the merriment until, having taken a dig at Petersen, he grunted, 'And now Tommy, it's your turn. When are you going to fight me?'

'So that's how you feel,' I exploded. 'I'll fight you now, out in the car-park. There's plenty of room. What about it. I'm not bluffing.'

Neusel went livid. Frank Godfrey, fearing an up-and-downer broke in, 'Now then boys, simmer down.'

Neusel snorted, and with, 'You are a funny man, Tommy Farr,' made himself scarce.

'Frank,' I said to Godfrey, 'I didn't mean a thing except to get inside his carcass. Now I know he's yellow. If he weren't he would know that I was only after getting his goat. We'll fight all right, if I have any say, and when we do put your loose change on Tommy Farr.'

Godfrey put on one of his famous 'special' cigars, and though he could not find speech, told me by his wide open eyes that he believed I was shouting my mouth off. For my part I was more than satisfied with the chance meeting with Neusel and I went back to Wales with him marked down next on my list.

I kept in useful training in 'Pandy, waiting for Max Baer to be put against Ben Foord. By way of keeping the two Baers full in the public eye, Buddy was given a fight with Jim Wilde some three weeks before Max was due to meet Ben. Buddy, as good tempered as he is huge, knocked out Wilde in the fourth round and went on to Swansea where he outpointed Jack London.

I was at the ringside to see Max Baer and Foord. It was a one-sided affair. Max gave Foord such a trouncing that the wonder was that Ben lasted until the ninth round. Foord took enough punishment to kill a normal man. I promised after beating Baer that I would give him a return match if Harringay were unable to find him another opponent, but Max, much to his own and my regrets, had news of the serious illness of his father, and he immediately packed for California.

Before he went away he sought me out to say that no man could have been better treated 'by your folk,' that 'they made me and Buddy one of themselves. Everybody's a sport here. How I wish I could stay on, but you know how it is, Tommy. Blood's thicker than water. I've got to be with Pop. Queer that a fighter should have a heart, I guess. But the guys who pay to see us thump or be thumped don't know, do they, Tommy.'

Max laughed his loudest, but he could not hide the tears that rolled down his tanned face. Oh yes, there is another, an intensely human side to the 'tom-fooling, playboy Max Baer'.

More I have to write of Max. That later.

CHAPTER 4

I had been back in Tonypandy only a few days after the Baer-Foord fight when I was asked to sign for a match with Neusel.

Instead of at once agreeing, Joby and I put on our thinking caps and by an assumed indifference spread an idea that we were not over-anxious to truck with the German. Would I fight Neusel? Of course I would, but . . . I kept Harringay guessing until it pleased me to discuss terms and, holding the trump card, I called high, so high that General Critchley did not mince words in telling me that I was a very difficult young fellow, which I didn't deny, but since it takes two to strike a bargain I stuck to my guns not caring a hoot what might be thought of me.

In the fight game, as in life, if you want anything you've got to pay for it. Harringay wanted me and I was determined that I would not sell except at my price. Let me say that Harringay were not in the least stingy: they paid me handsomely for what they set out to buy. I sold myself for a match with Neusel for £3500, and a nice present for myself. I was more than pleased, and after doing some arithmetic with Joby as the headmaster I decided that I

52

could well afford to use £1000 to back my chances. The market offered odds on Neusel.

I gambled so that if I won there would be round about £2000 in our kitty, apart from my end of the purse.

As against Baer I was given little more than an outside chance, which was understandable, for three times had Neusel stopped Jack Petersen and he had not been defeated in this country. 'Tommy Farr can box, but he is no puncher. Neusel will be too strong for him,' was the general line.

I was convinced that I could not only go the distance with Neusel, but that if I got on top he would curl up. That conviction was borne of the flare-up we had at the Star and Garter, and almost from the first day I started to train at Blackheath I declared I would win by a knockout, only to be twitted by leading assessors of values for cheekiness. The idea of me flattening Neusel was voted ridiculous.

None the less, I kept on blowing my trumpet. 'I'll be my own publicity agent,' I said to myself. 'Perhaps if I shout loud enough someone will sit up and take notice.' Of course I was wholly wrong, but under persistent knocking I had either to shout or blow up. Possibly I was more cocksure than discreet, but I developed such a frame of mind that soft-pedalling was beyond me. Besides, I had so tried myself out at Blackheath that I could find nothing physically or mentally wrong with me.

I remember as well as if it were last night, Sir Noel Curtis Bennet coming into my dressing-room as I waited to be called to the ring, asking how I felt. 'Tip-top,' I answered, 'I'm going to knock Neusel out.'

'Tommy,' warned Sir Noel, 'don't forget that Neusel is wonderfully strong and a tremendous puncher.'

'I tell you I'm going to knock him out,' I repeated with, I am afraid, some show of petulance.

'I hope so,' replied Sir Noel, 'but aren't you just a little over confident?'

'Not a bit,' I snapped. I was all on edge as may be supposed, for most times the hardest part of a fight is the seeming never-ending hours before the battle.

'Well good luck to you, Tommy,' called Sir Noel as he left to join his party at the ringside.

'Ready?' asked Tom Evans, as the whip put his inquiring head round the door and let in the blare of the fanfare. With Joby leading the way down the passage to the ring, I chatted with Tom Evans. What about, goodness knows. At any rate, it was no time for prattle or banter, but there's no accounting for what a man does to make him forget when he goes into action.

I was pleasantly jerked to the fullness of my senses by the crowd's ovation. 'Tommy,' it thundered. 'All London, all Wales is with you.' The cheers and shouts and screams of a mighty Welsh gallery was a reminder to avenge Jack Petersen.

I looked around and to my left I saw Ribbentrop [the German ambassador] laughing and joking, taking it for granted. I supposed that he was telling his lickspittlers what Neusel was under orders to do to me. The sight of him did me a power of good. 'You German dog,' I swore as he preened and posed.

I turned to Joby and asked him to tell my layers to bet an extra £100 that I would stop Neusel. For there was Neusel huddled on his seat, his straw head sunk in his chest, the picture of misery. And there was Paul Damski, about as comfortable as a cat on hot bricks.

When we were called to the centre of the ring Neusel

looked at the floor. As we made a show of shaking hands I spluttered, 'You've got your wish Walter – a fight with Tommy Far.'

'Joby,' I said to Churchill when I got back to my corner, 'I'm going all out to fight. It's got to be a knockout or nothing.'

'Perhaps you're right. Have your own way,' he allowed.

'Time, seconds out,' and I met a lumbering, slow-moving Neusel with a straight left that found the tip of his snub nose, and before he had time to sniff I banged a right to his ribs.

'Grab him, Walter,' yelled Damski, and Neusel clinched.

'Break,' commanded the referee. As Neusel stepped back I shot a left which landed below his eye, and then missed his jaw by a whisker with a right. I was outsmarting him at in-fighting, when the gong went for the end of the first round.

To a man the crowd was with me. Damski, bulging eyed, could not disguise his apprehension. I'll swear that the only man in the German camp who had not seen how definitely I had got on top was Ribbentrop.

At the start of the second round I feinted with my left and as Neusel dropped his guard I hooked him with a right on the chin. And as he struck out blindly by way of a reply I stung him on an already reddened nose. In obedience to the cries of Damski he clinched. I was glad, for then I could feel and hear him blowing, and I found it easy to handcuff him so that he could neither force me to carry his full weight nor get a single rib-bender home. I was the first to break but I was back into attack in a flash to find a clear road for my left hand, with which I prodded him almost as I pleased. A couple of rights with everything I had behind them shook him from tip to toe. When the end of the round was called I reckoned that I had made all the points.

If ever a man was minded to turn it up, it was Walter Neusel. I was positive that only the entreaties of Damski sent him into the third round. Remembering, as I do, vividly, I am certain that during the rest at the end of the second round Neusel decided that if he could not at once push back the tide, he would turn turtle. And Damski knew it.

Answering the call for the third round, I stepped in and scored, and hurt, with three straight lefts and followed with a right cross to the jaw. Neusel wobbled with punch drunkenness, and again I chinned him with a right. Stepping back, I hooked him on the jaw with a left and he dropped into a sitting position. Into his blue eyes there came a tell-tale mist. It was impossible to rise. To the frantic shouts of Damski to 'get up', he shook his head and with a wry face pointed to his knee. Damski, taking the hint, jumped into the ring, but not before the time-keeper had called 'Out', and Damski began massaging Neusel's leg by way of asking the crowd to believe that Walter had only been beaten by accident. He might have got away with it if Neusel had not straightened his face and got up unaided.

I knocked Neusel out: he did not lose because he was crippled. His exposure was complete, and whatever may be said to the contrary, he could not have lasted longer than he did.

If he were not out to the world when he went down in that third round then he proved himself to be an arrant coward. Ribbentrop must have been of that way of thinking, for no sooner had Neusel buckled up than he slunk away to be followed by those of his party he had brought to Harringay to witness the breaking up of the British champion.

I would have been genuinely sorry for Neusel if, with Damski, he had not squealed that he had been left with only one leg. You would have thought that since he would have it that a twisted leg beat him, he would have begged for a return match. He did nothing of the kind. He pocketed a generous purse, and maybe thanked his lucky stars that he had not been discovered for what he was at heart. I have it on good authority that during his stay in Britain he was paid anything up to £30,000.

It is fairly common knowledge that Paul Damski begged him to follow himself and Eric Seelig to the States, and like them, become an American citizen. But Neusel, though he saw his manager run out of Germany to escape a concentration camp, swore by the Nazis and two years after our fight bolted from London some twenty-four hours before the outbreak of war to join the German army.

If all I hear is true, Neusel, if he comes through [the war], will have to whistle for the fortune he salted away in the Berlin Bank. Different with Damski, who did not leave a single mark for the Jew-baiters. I should say that he is very well britched, and that Seelig, although he had more downs than ups in the American ring, is comfortably off.

After knocking out Neusel my ledger showed that I was so many thousands to the good that even frugal-minded Joby Churchill agreed that I had actually arrived in Easy Street. Yet it required a lot of persuasion to get him to approve of my squandering on a motor car and generally dress the part of British heavyweight champion. He too had become rich, thanks to his shrewd backing of me in each of the fights since taking the title from Foord. But there was emphatically no launching out for him. 'Tommy,' he said, 'we've both been through the mill. You feel posh if you like. I don't.

'I only know that I'm a damn sight better off than I was, but I'm still Joby Churchill. And I'm going to see that you keep both feet on the ground. The difference between having a good time, and burning up money, is the difference between happiness and sappiness; and that is a hell of a difference. Don't let money take you out of your depth. Less than six months ago you fought Rutz for £50. That was all the market would give you. What now? . . . For fighting Baer and Neusel, and throwing in presents and bets, you've raked in as near to £10,000 as makes no matter. And that money you are going to put in gilt-edge, else you and me will call it a day. Buy your motor car, spruce up, look around, but keep the shop open for customers. You've got lots to sell, and at a big profit.'

'Look you, Joby,' I begged, 'if you find me running loose, hit me on the head with a shovel.'

He threatened, 'It'll not be a shovel, it'll be a gun and a swell funeral.'

Further discussion was cut short by Sydney Hulls, who on behalf of Harringay, suggested a match with Max Schmeling. I went into conference with Ted Broadribb, and we agreed that, subject to terms, my next fight would be with the German champion. Articles were drawn up, and for a guarantee of £7000 I signed. Hulls, who had flown to and from Berlin several times to talk with Schmeling, induced Max to come to London, and the German gave his written word that he would fight me at Harringay on a date to be fixed.

I met Max at the offices of the Greyhound Association, where he was introduced to a gathering of the press. I found him a severe, silent man, much disposed to patronage. In signing us up, Hulls was highly commended (and deservedly) by General Critchley for bringing off a coup. And I was congratulated on getting the biggest guarantee ever given to a British boxer. There was back-slapping all round. I was feeling particularly good as I drove away in my car, bent on a holiday before settling down to training at Blackheath.

Schmeling took the first plane back to Berlin, where he was visited a few days later by Hulls. Then things began to happen.

Telephone and cable messages from New York warned us not to be too sure that Schmeling would toe the mark, that he had in fact only signed for a fight with me to force Mike Jacobs to match me for the world title with Joe Louis. And that if Jacobs said the word, Max would beat it to New York and leave me high and dry. If I was quick to suspect, it was because experience, bitter and often cruel, had taught me that in the fight game nothing might be taken for granted.

I was promised in black and white that before and after Schmeling had contracted to fight me, he was pressing Jacobs to put me in the ring with Louis. It was very disturbing. It needed all the tact and diplomacy of Joby Churchill to stop me asking for a showdown.

'Tommy,' said Joby, 'let us suppose that Schmeling is playing poker, with yourself as a full house to Jacobs's two pairs. The cards are not on the table yet. Until they are, do and say nothing.'

There was no denying the wisdom of Joby, and I went down to Eastbourne to compete my car in a *concourse d'élégance*. I was fortunate enough to win first prize, and, as proud as Lucifer, I joined a luncheon party at the leading hotel of the town.

'Mr Tommy Farr,' a page sang. I called, 'Here you are, sonny.'

'You are wanted in the lounge.'

Breaking away from the party, I found Broadribb, Paul Damski, Jeff Dickson and others who didn't seriously count.

'What's the big idea?' I asked.

'Tommy,' said Broadribb, 'I want you to meet Sol Strauss – he's here representing Mike Jacobs.'

'This,' I told myself, 'is where you put your best side out.'

For once, I have since been reminded, I played the part of a gentleman. I smiled with all the geniality I could muster to Strauss, who cupped his ear, by way of advertising his deafness. I bade him welcome, and wished him well. He gave me a hearty handshake and fixed me with a steely eye, the while he chewed an unlighted cigar. In an aside to Dickson and Damski he drawled, 'I expected to see something different, a roughneck, after what I've heard.' Then to me, 'I'm mighty glad to see you.' We all went up to my suite.

'Mr Strauss,' I broke in, 'I'd like to see you alone.' And to a much surprised company, I took him by the arm and steered him into my bedroom, which I locked. Instinct told me that the old man, who I found out was Mike Jacobs's lawyer, was a friend to whom I could talk freely.

He opened, 'I'm here to sign you for a fight with Joe Louis, for the world heavyweight title, nothing less.'

'Not so fast,' I spluttered. 'Come into the bathroom, away from listeners-in.' I was taking no chances with the redskins, so I bolted the door.

'You know,' I explained, 'that I am signed to fight Schmeling.'

'Listen Tommy,' he hastened, 'I know all about it. That's why I'm here. I want you to believe that Max will run out on you if he can dragoon Mike Jacobs into matching him for the championship. A clever guy, Max. He figures that rather than Jacobs keeping Louis in pickle indefinitely, he'll give him his price to fight Joe. Now Mike ain't a guy to be a stand for a hold up, or the least suspicion of blackmail. Max has told the world that he is being frozen out of the championship. That's just plain hokum. He was offered a title fight with Louis on what Jacobs reckoned were fair terms. He refused, being sure that Mike would stump up so as to carry on his summer programme.'

'You swear on your honour that Schmeling is playing fast and loose?' I asked.

'Dead sure.'

'And I can have a title fight?'

'Nothing surer.'

'In that case I'm yours if you promise to look after me. How much for my end?'

'Fifty thousand dollars in sterling.'

I pinched myself all over to make certain that I had heard Sol Strauss alright, and then rejoined Broadribb and the rest of the company. Ted of course, knew what Strauss wanted. We looked over the position from all angles and decided to close with Jacobs. We held the view that although Schmeling had contracted to fight me he would make any sacrifice to get Louis.

It was notorious that, having stopped Joe in a non-title bout, he was sure that, given the opportunity, he could and would take the title from him. And we did not forget that if Schmeling rated, I would not only be £7000 light, but there was no telling where my next opponent would come from.

Petersen was definitely off the map, Foord eclipsed, Baer gone home, and we put Jack Doyle completely out of the court. If the Boxing Board of Control had had any jurisdiction over Schmeling, it would have been different . . .

To Max, a contract was just a scrap of paper to tear up if it suited his purpose. And so we closed with Strauss who, wise old bird, scented legal troubles and suggested that I go with him to Paris to escape a possible injunction and to sail to New York from Cherbourg.

A plane was chartered and across the Channel we flew. Strauss saw to it that once he had got me in Paris I would have no time to fall homesick. I was taken everywhere and made dizzy. Luncheon, tea parties, dinners, introductions galore. And at my hotel, flowers from a famous actress; which flowers, carefully carded, I discovered afterwards were bought and sent by Strauss, fox that he was. I had an idea that Jeff Dickson took no small part in the game of kid and cod 'em. They certainly had me believe that all Paris had fallen for Tommy Farr. I did meet many notabilities, both sexes. And in the merry-go-round I was introduced to Laval [French politician who had been prime minister 1935–6] and Count Ciano [Italian Foreign Minister, son-in-law to Mussolini] at a reception to which a 'special' invitation was engineered for me. Whether Ciano warmed to me I cannot say, but he assured me that he was a regular fight fan.

'I saw you beat the big Baer, and afterwards give the knockout to Neusel. And I shall never forget what you did to Primo Carnera; he was no good at all.'

How that toad Ciano could lie. I did not fight Carnera, and I doubt whether he saw me in any fight at all.

Entirely happy I would've been with good honest, hard-swearing Joby to take me out of the whirl of Paris. It was not possible to send more than a skeleton message that I was OK. Strauss saw that I was never lost sight of morning, noon or night. I was a man without a soul to call his own. I was terribly homesick. There was no turning back, even if I wanted to do so. America was a country I had read about. To be privileged to fight for the world heavyweight title within a year of a £50 fight with Rutz, I could scarcely credit.

'Tommy,' I often heard myself muttering, 'there's a catch in it. It's not true.'

CHAPTER 5

I was thankful indeed when we took train to Cherbourg and set sail for New York, as was Strauss and the rest.

The first thing I did after leaving France was to radio to the wondering members of my family and Joby Churchill that everything was top-hole. During every hour of the crossing I tried and failed to picture myself in New York. Puzzlement and the heat of my cabin denied me restful sleep which I needed badly after hectic Paris: and in between turnings and tossings I wondered what London was saying and thinking.

It is not possible to describe my innermost feelings as we sailed into New York harbour. I was entranced: nothing that I imagined fitted in with that I beheld: the incredible skyscrapers rooted me to the upper deck upon which I stood. It was all fantastic, overpoweringly strange, weird, uncanny, intoxicating, pulverizing; unreal, yet real: and I would have gone on and on drinking in and feasting upon a truly wonderful and magical transformation . . . Tony-pandy with it's one street that mattered, and now New York . . . but 'Hello, Tommy Farr' stopped my dreaming.

The newspaper boys had arrived and good and proper

did they put me through the third degree, while battalions of cameras clicked. There was no waiting for answers to the questions they fired at me: they supplied the answers, to say nothing of the wisecracks, mostly at my expense. In my greyness I decided I was being razzed and gaffed. So I loosened up. That started the roasting and boiling of me: I was 'cocky' and worse. To put it mildly I did not get a good press. That, however, was because I did not understand.

But I am going too fast. There is a meeting with Mike Jacobs about which I must tell.

I was taken to him after interviews and broadcast at the quayside and endless snapshots. I found him in his office at his Twentieth-Century Club. For all the privacy it allowed it might have been pitched on the sidewalk, which as it happened was being torn up by pneumatic drills; to complete the pandemonium the overhead railway rattled unceasingly.

For all the notice Jacobs took of the din he might have been operating in a cloister. On his desk that seemed to be in a hopeless state of confusion was a forest of telephones, which apparently took to ringing without the slightest provocation.

'Come right in, Tahmmy,' Mike rasped as I stood at attention at the swing gate of his office. 'Mighty glad to see you.'

He was coatless, for the day was choking hot. His neck-tie, the noisiest ever, was hit off by a giant safety pin, his false teeth rattled. From his bottom lip a stump of a cigarette dangled. His little eyes twinkled and danced as, giving me the 'once-over', he guessed 'we better get together.'

For a moment I could not reconcile him with the great Uncle Mike, czar of the American ring. I could only see

him as a quaint waddling, generously nosed little man,
dressed anyhow. First impressions were entirely wrong.
There was something about him that I cannot explain, a
something at once baffling yet convincing. He got to the
root of things like a knife. He was without nonsense. I
became his captive long before our first interview was
ended. His frankness forbade questions or quibbles.

'Listen Tahmmy,' he said, 'I want you to have everything you want. I know how you feel. Mighty strange, eh?
Get around for a few days and if you have any trouble
come to your Uncle Mike. You've got your big chance.
Make the most of it. Good luck and plenty.'

We were fixed up at the Alamac Hotel with a bedroom
for me on the 24th floor. The heat was terrific and what
with sleeping so high up and food altogether different from
what I was accustomed, I began to wilt. It had been tenta-
tively arranged that I should train in or near the city. I
told Jacobs that I much feared that I would not be able to
settle down in New York, I wanted to work as far away
from crowds as possible.

'That's easy,' comforted Mike, and quarters were found
at Long Branch some fifty miles out on the Atlantic shore.
It suited me down to the ground. There I could breath and
concentrate.

The mayor, Mr Alton Evans, a good Welshman, ordered
out the band to greet me and gave me the freedom of his
city. A large private residence was placed at my disposal.
I did my training at a sports ground a few hundred yards
away. Nearby across the road was the West End Casino
and swimming-pool of which I was made an honorary
member. I wanted for nothing in the way of accommo-
dation. It was training de luxe: a well appointed gym,
countryside ideal for roadwork. The only fault I had to

find was that the ring in the open air was too large – twenty-
six feet, if you please. In sparring it made me look an
especially slow mover, which critics almost without exception did not forget to enlarge upon.

In our mansion there were housed and fed in addition
to myself, Ted Broadribb, who was later joined by his wife,
George Daly, Bob Scally, Tom Evans, Babe Cullen and
Jerry Casale, who as my bodyguard, was employed by Mike
Jacobs. Jerry, known as 'the Gunman' (and I should say
he was lightning quick on the trigger) never allowed me
out of sight. Woe betide gatecrashers. A great character
was Jerry. No everyday bouncer: he had the key to all
problems. He would perhaps not pass as a master of tact;
he was just Jerry Casale with all the answers to all the
questions. He played no small part in helping to get the
two Baers out of a jam and bringing them over to Britain.
The 'boys' here will remember 'Jerry the Gunman' more
than somewhat.

My early days at Long Branch were so mapped out that
social calls came before hard work. If I had accepted all
the hospitality offered me there would have been no fight.
Every house was an open house. Of toffee nosed high-hats
there were none, and though at first I was shy to accept
invitations from swell folk I was made so much at home
that even afternoon tea with a millionairess and talks with
her on psychology did not seem out of place. A gracious,
understanding lady she was.

'You might think it odd,' she said, 'that I should profess
interest in prize-fighting. I have never seen a fight. I asked
you to call upon me so that I can the better understand
why and how men come to be prize-fighters. Now I have
found out, for you have told me your life story and I
find that prize-fighter and everyday business man is but a

difference in labels: actually they are one and the same, both are fighters.'

The other side of my stay and experiences at Long Branch by way of the opening chapters to my training, the newspaper boys made me out to be every sort of a guy that I wasn't. When I complained to Mike Jacobs that I was being put in the bad, all I got back was, 'It's good publicity. It doesn't matter a hoot what them newspaper guys write so long as they keep you in the news. That's their job, steaming up. It don't mean a thing if they bring in the cash customers. Take on a thicker skin, Tahmmy.'

'But,' I protested, 'there is surely a limit.'

'There ain't,' snapped Mike.

I was not of that way of thinking. Especially when almost daily I read statements that I would not dream of making. That I was resentful of the bargers-in; that I often went off the deep end and rubbed the writers up the wrong way, I confess. It was because of my ignorance of American methods.

If I was seen alone with one of the bathing pool beauties I was speeding for the marriage market. In print, in pictures, I was engaged times without number. But what really got my goat were the fellows who burst upon me with, 'They tell me you are sure to beat Joe Louis. Guess we'd like to know how it's got to be done.'

Then I would see red. Hence 'Cocky Tommy Farr' . . . 'The Limey says he'll put one over on Joe' . . . 'Tommy Farr sweats on the top line with temper'. Most galling and discouraging was a London writer who would have folks at home believe that I would be as good as beaten before I took the ring.

As a reply to cheapeners I bet £500 at 2–1 against me.

But it was no use. I was still rated little higher than an outsider.

Thankful to goodness I was indeed when Joby Churchill with his son Billy, with whom I fought as a boy, arrived at Long Branch. 'What's this?' the newspaper writers asked, in a chorus of laughter, 'A page from Dickens?'

How Joby found his way from teeming New York without being mobbed was beyond me. But there he was, the very same Joby Churchill, come thousands of miles to stand at the ready, to help me fight the battle of my life, challenging, defiant.

'Jerry the Gunman', in choicest Bowery, called out to Babe Cullen to 'come meet the old man of the sea'. Babe shot through the corner of his mouth to the chef, 'See what's washed up on the beach', and away he rushed to bring the newshawks from the nearby press camp. So it was that in a twinkling Joby was served up as red-hot news.

'The Druid at Long Branch,' 'Captain Cuttle comes to life', 'The wooden legged Bard from Tonypandy is here'. Such was the introduction of the good Joby to America.

It was left to Dan Parker, the famous columnist, to reproduce Joby as he walked down the gangway of the *Queen Mary* 'to stagger New York'.

'Tommy Farr', he wrote, 'may be knocked for a homer by Joe Louis, but he has already done more than any fighter; he has sent for and produced all alive and kicking, from his native Tonypandy, the answer to a columnist's prayer – Joby Churchill, a little Welsh-speaking man straight from the mountains. He's no swell guy; you take him or leave him, as you please. And that goes for Tommy Farr too.

'Joby was through the customs in the tick of a clock. He carried all his belongings in a satchel no bigger than a day-tripper's luncheon basket – a spare suit, second pair of boots, four shirts at the most, each the same colour and of such practical length as to serve as nightgowns. One collar completes his outfit.

'Knowing old bird; it was a rubber collar that asks no more than a daily shower to be all cleaned up and ready for wear.

'His only outward show of extravagance is a gold watch-chain which permits no escape. You'll laugh when you see him, but Joby's no sucker; he's a wise guy, no innocent abroad, I'm telling you. He's different, a breath of mountain air.'

To all of which Joby asked, 'What did they expect? A cross between a sheep and a goat?'

'Joby,' I answered, 'you are what you are, Joby Churchill, the best pal of all.'

During the first week at Long Branch, 'getting acquainted' was my especial job. Visitors came in an endless stream from everywhere. Good sportsmen, curiosity mongers, mischief makers. Down the street was an 'army of occupation'. Writers, artists, manufacturers of scoops. There was the telephone with a licence to ring and ting-a-ling day and night, an ever swelling fan mail, mascots by the score, testimonial getters, an epidemic of autograph hunters, brass-faced spongers.

Mike Jacobs installed his own publicity man on my doorstep at an ambassadorial salary. Wherever I went, whatever I said, was duly reported. If in an interview I ventured to say something more than commonplace, I was a 'fresh guy'. If I questioned the veracity of a story, I was drubbed for squawking. I could do little or nothing right.

I was denied the least privacy. How I longed for the

quiet homeliness of Blackheath. 'Jerry,' I asked Casale, 'tell me how to get into the good. What's wrong with me, anyway?'

'Tommy,' he replied as he sat on the front porch, shaving a chunk of wood with a murderous knife, 'a fighter ain't supposed to have opinions of his own. So when you ups and tells the newspaper guys that you haven't come all the way from Tonypandy to be licked by the champ, they just don't get you. They think you're either loco or have never heard of Joe Louis. Forget it. You see, Tommy, you're not what they expected to find, some kind of mouse. They ain't got you and you ain't got them: that's all there is to it. Phil Scott is the only British heavyweight they've seen and he set no one alight.

'If you read, and I'm betting you will, that you're a "ham", "cheese" or "palooka", keep all your wool on. For that's how it most times goes in the game as played by the fellahs paid to hand out the dope. Let them have a Tommy Farr basinful, if and when you like, but for the love of Mike don't get held up. Remember, you are on show, and being a Limey you've got to be steamed up. How the steaming is done cuts no ice.

'You'll find after you've fought the champ, your roasters and boilers will be your rooters.'

With my card expertly marked by Jerry, I managed to bed down reasonably well, without winning the full approval of the critics or being spared disturbing ripples in my own immediate circle. Whatever the rifts in the family, however, they were more than counter balanced by the readiness with which I acclimatized.

Throughout my training the weather was terrifically hot, now blistering, again choking. So far as I can recollect there was not a single day that I felt seedy. I was out and about before the sun was up and revelled in road work, now sprinting, again jog-trotting and skipping and shadow-boxing as I went along. In the gym I wanted for nothing to ensure complete physical fitness.

My first concern was to be sure of my legs. I kept slavishly to pre-arranged plans and I did not lack for sparring partners, among whom was Abe Feldman, who eight months previously had defeated John Henry Lewis, who had been light-heavyweight champion of the world until he was forced to retire owing to damaged eyes. Other helpers in addition to Bob Scally and George Daly were Basher Dean, Joe Wagner and Roscoe Manning. I also boxed with Natie Brown, who had twice fought Louis.

Jack Dempsey was one of the early visitors to Long Branch. He offered 'a few friendly hints to victory'.

'Jack,' said I, 'I am much obliged for your advice, which I prize highly. But I'm going to fight my own way, according to the needs of the moment.'

'Some guy,' Dempsey sang out to a crowd who had gathered around. 'I like him. He believes in himself, not because he's cocky, but because he feels what he says.' And to various newspaper boys who asked for his opinion of my boxing, Dempsey added, 'Farr has a good left hand and it bites, it does more than score points. There's a big healthy shoulder behind it and I should think it is the best that Louis will have to meet.

'This for sure: he can box and if he can move around as well as they say, I guess Joe will get a shock. He's the kind of guy who would not blink if the roof fell in. He may not beat the champ but my first impressions kill stone dead the idea that British heavyweights are given to fright.

'He's just as likely to spring a surprise as some of the

others – Braddock when he beat Baer and Schmeling in licking Louis.'

A deal of fault was found with me because I did not reduce sparring to out-and-out fighting. I took the view, and will ever be of that way of thinking, that the open road to fighting completeness is not to be found in hammering the life out of sparring partners.

Training, to be helpful, must be of physical, mental and educational value. A knockout in the gym is not proof of quality. The test of a fighter is in the public ring, not in his workshop.

I knocked none of my partners over or under the ropes at Long Branch, not because I wished to be credited with having something up my sleeve, but largely for the reason that I was determined to preserve as far as was humanly possible two perfectly sound fists. On the other hand, I encouraged the other fellow to punch with everything he had: my purpose was to see that his punches did not land with all the weight put into them and at the same time work out the kind of problems that would be set by Louis.

Before and after going into camp, I made a searching study of cinema-pictured Louis, in his more important fights. And I trained with every care so as to meet the demands that I knew would be asked of me.

In a spar with Wagner, my eye was cut. Nothing serious, but the mishap was served up as something of a sensation and Commissioner Bill Brown and Doc Walker hot-footed to Long Branch to judge the nature of the injury for themselves. They were more than pleased to report that there was nothing seriously amiss.

Dempsey promised to put the gloves on with me. He compromised by inducing me to take a day off and go to New York, where, as a publicity stunt, I was photographed alongside Red Burman, a fighter in whom Jack was financially interested. Next break from the grindstone I spent in a holiday camp for crippled children. In stories and songs I took them over my native mountains and through the valleys. And they hip-hipped and hoorayed and hummed and strummed catchy little melodies, to force a confession that never greater fighters than they. Two hundred or more of them, white, black, yellow boys, sorely crippled, yet world beaters every one of them. The pitiable slums from which they had come forgotten; it was enough that, for one whole week, the sea and sun and air were their very own, and I was made glad and refreshed by an unforgettable lesson in fortitude.

Among the regulars at Long Branch was Dick Griffen, a little middle-aged man, who's fighting career was cut short by blindness at a moment when he was heading for bantam championship honours. He came all the way from Dallas, Texas. With him was his wife, who served as his eyes. I was being massaged by Tom Evans when he was brought to me by his lady who, without the least palaver, explained that her husband 'who does quite a spot of promoting these days, back home, would be just tickled to know you.'

'I guess,' said Griffen, 'that I must tell you what I think about your boxing. I sure like it. Sounds funny coming from an old-timer who can't see, but just the same I know what you can do and how you do it. My pard here knows all the answers in the fight game and with her by my side, which I reckon is always, I can tell the guy that you are. You've got my OK. Go to it and all the luck. I'll be there to see you. I've not missed a big fight since an unlucky blow brought on blindness and through the little missus I have seen them as clearly as if I had my eyes. And I say, that was a corking right-hander that put Feldman down just now. I could feel it was a smasher. It was a half-arm shot, wasn't it? You see, the wife and I have a code of our own by which I know exactly what is happening, whether it's clever footwork, straight punching, a swinger, or what not. I guess you don't punch as hard as the champ, but, no kidding, you're a boxer after my own heart.'

And on those days that followed during my training, there was the sightless warrior at the ringside, waiting for my wave of the hand by way of greeting. And he would smile as I waved, as if to say, 'I'm watching you, Tommy Farr.'

I wait impatiently to redeem a promise to visit him and his good lady in their home town. When last I heard of him he was still getting around in good shape, both in health and pocket.

A red-letter day for me was the coming of a party of Welshmen, a trip load of them, to Long Branch. The mayor, Mr Evans, to mark the occasion, presented me with the Welsh flag and there was the singing of *Land of My Fathers*, with myself as leader of the choir. I was no longer lonely; I was with my own folk again.

But Max and Buddy Baer arrived and there developed something of a shindy, to the great joy of the news hawks, ravenous for something with a kick in it.

I had finished my sparring and was about to do some skipping when Max bounded into the ring, the soul of cheeriness. He made to slap me on the back, as he breezed, 'Hello Tommy.'

I refused a proffered hand. Before you could say 'Jack Robinson', Ted Broadribb, Tom Evans and others were in the ring to stop a possible dust-up. It was explained to an astonished Max that I had strongly resented a statement given to a New York reporter upon his arrival from California, that I had butted him to defeat at Harringay. Max swore that he had said no such thing and we shook hands.

Now for letting the cat out of the bag: the 'scene' was acted by arrangement for the sake of publicity. Mike Jacobs, the old fox, thought it would be a great idea if the news boys were given something fresh. Measured by space, the incident certainly did the trick. Whether it brought in the cash customers I can only guess. Max thought it as a huge joke: for myself, unversed as I was in the higher art of publicity, I was not sure.

The Baers, with their manager Hoffman, took quarters in the neighbourhood and Buddy, who had come to fight Abe Simon in a curtain-raiser to my battle with Louis, did his work in my ring after I had done my daily sparring.

Roughly a couple of weeks before the fight it was arranged that, together with Louis, I should show myself at New Jersey in fighting clobber, for pictures. I was on the spot in good time. Louis kept me waiting for at least a quarter of an hour. When he appeared I jolted him with, 'Joe, I'd almost given you up. Been hiding, eh?' I could feel his eyes giving me the once-over and noticing that his attention was riveted on my back, which had been cut and slashed when I was working in the pits, I asked, 'Joe, what's got you?'

'Tahmmy,' he drawled, 'what's dem cuts about youse?'

'Oh them,' I replied. 'I used to wrestle with tigers in a circus.'

'Gee,' sighed Joe. 'They tell me you are a tough guy, but I never knew you fought tigers and wrestled snakes. Youse sure tough all right.'

From that day – our first meeting, by the way – until he

climbed into the ring at the Yankee Stadium, Joe wondered what he would bump against.

I don't pretend that I got him scared, but I did make him strangely curious.

CHAPTER 6

I was enormously pleased with myself when I had put the finishing touches to my preparation. I could not have been fitter or more confident. Odds against me shortened appreciably.

I told Joby Churchill to bet any amount that I would go the distance and to place a last minute bet at three to one against me that I would win. My last words to a crowd of interviewers were: 'It is because I've got to the top by my own efforts that I shall win. I have not jumped to the front. I have gone one better each time out.

'I have backed myself for more money than I have made out of all my fights up to twelve months ago. I shall go out to do or die, and I shall not die. I've never been scared: It's me or Louis "for it".'

The weigh-in was at the State Commission building, New York, and with bodyguard Jerry the Gunman, manager, trainer and various members of the Long Branch staff, I presented myself according to schedule, as did Joe Louis. Overnight there was heavy rain, but the weather was fine when we set out for New York. The weighing-in room was crowded to suffocation, the noise ear-splitting. I had to scrummage a way to the scales. I weighed 207 lbs. A seemingly bewildered Louis turned the beam at 198 lbs. I was surprised that I went so much more than Louis. That, however, was a detail.

Mike Jacobs, bursting in upon the crowd yelled, 'Boys, the fight's postponed until Monday.'

'Why?' was shouted.

'Because,' snapped Jacobs, 'there can't be no fight until Monday.'

That was that. There was nothing for it but to return to Long Branch. Louis did not say a word: he was led away to be motored back to Pompton Lakes, where he had his camp.

It was spread around that the breakdown in the weather was responsible for the hold-up. Mike Jacobs's till showed no more than £43,000 in the locker. Mike banked on £60,000, nothing less, of which Louis was to receive 40 per cent, the Milk Fund 10 per cent, and myself £10,000. Jacobs could not understand why the fight had not captured the popular imagination. I could have told him the reason. His literary boosters had persisted in writing me down, and when they mounted a horse of another colour it was too late to repair the damage. From Jacobs's point of view it was as well that he blamed the weather, for on the new date, the Saratoga races would be over, and the regulars would be free to go to the fight.

I was feeling pretty sick because of the postponement and glad I was to be back in my house at Long Branch, to calm the storm that raged within me. The tempest was soon over, however.

'It cannot be,' I forced myself to believe, 'that four days longer will make a fatal difference. At any rate Louis is in the same boat, and why should the hold up affect me more than him?'

I was thankful that the press camp had been disbanded and that the public try-outs were at an end.

Joby Churchill said, 'Things may not seem to be running our way, but I'm thinking that it's all for the best. I know how you feel inside. There's nothing more terrible that waiting to go over the top, but you must thank your lucky stars that you've come through all the weeks of training without a mishap, and if, as you say, you're OK upstairs, there is no fear that your sharp edges will be blunted. Now listen, you'll be all the better if you get off a pound or two.'

I agreed and did such long spells of skipping that I shed every particle of superfluous flesh I carried and got down to just a trifle more than fourteen stone (196 lbs), a weight I was sure suited me entirely.

I was in the highest feather when I went for the second weigh-in, but, to put it mildly, I was not a little ruffled when Commissioner Brown warned me that I would be fired out of the ring if I butted.

'Get this, Mr Commissioner,' I told him, 'there's none of the mountain goat in me. I've come here to fight Joe Louis. Yes, all the way from Tonypandy, and I shall fight as I've always fought, fair and square. There'll be no butting by me.'

'Don't get sore, Tahmmy,' begged the Commissioner, 'I'm just telling you, that's all.'

'All the same,' I cut him short, 'I don't like it.'

With that I dressed, sung out 'I'll be seeing you Joe,' to Louis as he left the room in the charge of his minders, and gave myself over to Jerry Casale, who steered me through a non-stop talking crowd to be driven away in a waiting motor car. My hide-out in New York was our secret and was so well kept that I might have been a hundred miles from the city instead of resting within a mile or so from the stadium.

There was no talking fight except by Churchill and myself and we spoke in Welsh, and what we had to say had most to do with reckoning as to how we stood in the matter of bets. The old fellow had so speculated that barring being knocked out, I would win a small fortune.

'Joby,' I whispered, 'let's chance another couple of hundred, if, as there is certain to be, there's betting on each round. Louis will only stop me by a fluke. I'm going all the way, nothing surer.'

'Let's see,' calculated Joby, 'up to now you've backed yourself with every penny of £1500, at all kinds of odds, but I'm with you that we might as well be killed for a sheep as a lamb. Another couple of hundred wouldn't break us anyway. Besides, when a fellow is chancing his own money he fights the better.'

Joby so allowed his money sense to run riot as to provide just the distraction I needed. And there were games of cards at which I won consistently. Time passed with refreshing pleasantness. I was able to get a spell of soothing sleep, and after an early evening meal we set out on the short journey to the Yankee Stadium.

I was much encouraged by the warm ovation given me as I drove through the gates of the famous arena. And when, dressed for the battle, I went from my dressing-room into the stadium, to take a seat at the ringside for the end of one of the preliminary bouts, I was cheered loud and long. If I had been 100 per cent American, I could not have expected a warmer-hearted greeting. To Joby, who sat by my side, I said. 'This is like a draft of champagne.

I couldn't have believed it. I thought they would only have eyes and shouts for the champion. Joby, we've got the folk here all wrong. They are going out of their way to guarantee that I shall have a square deal.'

Let me say that I have never appeared before a finer sporting crowd than the some 60,000 who gathered at the Yankee Stadium on the night of 31 August 1937, and paid round about £50,000 to see me fight Louis for the heavyweight championship of the world. No more compelling sight have I beheld than that crowd that came from far and wide to tell of every phase of life. I am without the gift to reproduce in words the picture painted by that mighty throng.

On the opposite side of the ring from where I sat was Gene Tunney, with his millionaire party. Jack Dempsey was his near neighbour. Politicians, towering Wall St personalities, world famous cinema stars, celebrated writers, the one and only Babe Ruth, tennis cracks, foremost golfers, anybody who was anybody had a place in the vast congregation. Old-timers, one of whom was Jack Johnson, all the champions, past and present, had been rounded up by Mike Jacobs. Never was a prize-ring so dressed.

'Tommy,' nudged Joby, to bring me back to earth, 'if they keep you sitting here much longer staring and dreaming, you'll either get the shivers or forget all about your job.'

I am bound to say that it would have been better if I had been kept in the dressing-room longer. I was lightly clad, and though the night air was warm there was a deal of humidity in it. Happily I was neither wearied of waiting (so much was there to see and drink in) nor was I any the worse for the long wait for the call to the ring. None the

Joe Louis visiting Tommy in his Brighton house.

Previous page: Tommy Farr's whole life revolved around his fight and subsequent relationship with the great Joe Louis. Farr thought he had done enough to win, as did many pundits, but the record book shows that after 15 rounds the fight was awarded to Louis on points.

oe Louis and Tommy in London, 12 January, 1973.

Leonard Trievnor, *Daily Express*

Training at the Sussex CCC Ground in the early 1950's.
The temptation to make a come-back proved too difficult for Tommy to resist.

Training at Brighton for his come back fight against Jan Klein at Pontypridd on 7 September 1950

The Inseparable Couple.   Tommy with a picture he sent to Monty in April, 1940.
Twentieth Century Studios

Monty to Tommy
Kriston Roger.

Right: Tommy with son Gary.
Sussex Photo Agency

Below: Christmas Day, 1984 Hidden Hills, California.

less, I was glad when I was free to duck under the ropes. I was given a rousing reception.

Louis was quickly to hand, but before we were called together by the referee Arthur Donovan for instructions, there was a parade of champions, introductions, announcements and the thumping of Jacobs's big drum. In my corner were Ted Broadribb, Tom Evans, Babe Cullen and, most important to me, Joby Churchill, who had not only both my ears, but, unofficially, was my adviser-in-chief. I know of no more intelligent, or so helpful a reader of a fight than Joby.

I have often been asked how I felt when, to the roar of the biggest crowd before whom I had ever appeared, I strode into the centre of the ring, at the command of Arthur Donovan. I was keyed to the highest pitch, but, believe it or not, I was in full possession of my wits. And no butterflies fluttered in my belly. I was tense, of course, but emphatically not nervous. Call it cocksuredness if you will. But deep down in me was an unshakeable belief that I should win. I could see and think with every straightness.

In that blaze of light I stood with Louis, almost toe to toe, listening to Donovan's hurried explanation of the rules. Joe gave not the slightest sign of comprehension. For all the emotion he showed he might have been made of bronze. but make no mistake, Louis, though perhaps slow on the uptake, is capable of doing his own thinking. A dumb-bell? Not on your life. It would be more apt to describe him as a strong, silent man, not a little shy, definitely hateful of fuss and mouthers and cheapjacks.

Physically, he comes splendidly near to perfection.

But the fight.

The gong, 'Seconds out'.

'Now or never,' I called to Joby as I went to meet Louis,

who came all in a hurry from his corner to the centre of the ring, his carriage and general arrangements such as to have it supposed that he had been taught and moulded by British masters. I crouched and weaved to so set him guessing that he opened a way for my left hand, which I planted on his nose. He shot out a right which I dodged, and jumping into the attack I again scored with the left. Joe back-pedalled, but I resisted a temptation to get close.

Louis also played for safety, and with both of us more intent upon scoring points than exploding fireworks, that first round was colourless. The crowd clamoured for action. I was more than satisfied when I went back to my corner. I had need to be, for I had got in front.

'Joby,' I ventured to Churchill, 'I can box better than Louis, and I'll take him places he's not been before.'

Louis came jog-trotting into the second round, obviously for a kill. I beat him to the punch, but without pulling him up in his tracks, and he fired a classic left-hander that caught me under the eye. Instead of letting go his right, as I expected and for which I was prepared, he jabbed with his left without doing more than stinging me. At any rate I did not break ground. The contrary: I shuffled and dodged into the inside position and belted Joe's body good and hard. I finished with a left hook that made him sniff.

In answer to coloured Jack Blackburn, his chief second, Louis tried to cross me with a vicious right but I swayed clear, only to be cuffed with his left. Louis, in obedience to shouted instructions, went all out for a knockout, but remained baffled by the awkwardness of my stance and my bobbing and weaving. His right-handed shots misfired. I reckoned that he did no more than share the honours of that second round, and as I studied him during the interval, I decided that he was far from happy.

Joby whispered that the betting boys were beginning to hedge. I was feeling fine and dandy – more confident than ever.

But . . . in the infancy of the third round, when in a fair way of luring Louis into a false position, I half slipped, and he let go a regular shower of blows. I rode most of them but he cut both my eyes. The crowd yelled for Joe to 'finish him', and with blood streaming from my slashed eyes it must have seemed that my goose was more than three parts cooked. How I cursed my luck. For I was as strong as a bull, chock full of fight, with peepers sorely damaged and threatening to close tight. Nevertheless, I held hard to wits and guns, which I fired into the stomach of Joe, and forced him to box at a distance.

I must have appeared a hopeless case when the bell sounded at the end of the session. Twelve more rounds were called for, and there I was with half-shut eyes and a blood-painted face.

I said to Churchill, as he watched an overwrought Broadribb stop the bleeding, 'If I am not blinded I shall pull through. So long as I can see him, Joe will not knock me out. He's tried to do it, God knows, and failed. I'll take all he has. Bank on that.'

Joby smiled encouragement. Little did he know that midway in the round, a finger of my right hand had been injured to breaking point. This is what had happened. The finger had caught in a piece of loose cotton in my glove and when I punched it was put out of joint. But I would have died rather than tell the old soldier of the injury.

In all the rounds that followed I succeeded in hiding the accident, though I suffered dreadful pain.

It is quite beyond me to explain how I gave as much as I received until the seventh round, when Louis, with the pole-axe which he stacked in either hand, crashed me on the jaw and ripped into my ribs. The crowd jumped and roared. I have heard tell that one London newspaper man was so sure that I would go down and out that he picked up his writing pad in readiness to bolt to his New York office. But a fight is never over until it is won.

To shouts of 'You've got him, Joe', I wriggled away from the ropes of a neutral corner, to which I'd been pinned, and gave blow for blow. More than that, I forced Louis on the retreat, and brought an ugly lump up under his eye. The round ended with me attacking furiously, and to much purpose, and to the shouts of 'Good boy, Tommy' from the thousands who looked on amazed that I was not only strong on my legs, but showed no signs of quitting. Truth was, that in stemming the tide I drew upon my strength almost to the last dregs, and yet whether because of mulishness or pride (perhaps a combination of both) I clung to a certainty that a points victory for Louis was the most he could hope for.

I did not go flop in my corner when the end of the round was clanged. I sat down in a perfectly normal way. My major troubles were my shutting eyes, and the finger into which was crowded an army of devils.

Reaching for and wiping my liver-coloured face with a sponge, Broadribb said, 'You look like taking a dive, Tommy.'

I squirmed. Joby Churchill, who heard this, let loose a few choice words, which fortunately for all concerned were in Welsh, and were not understood, except by myself and Tom Evans. Otherwise there would have been a rumpus.

'Taking a dive, if you please,' I said to myself. I was stung to the quick.

As if to heap coals on an already raging fire, the collodion used to stop the blood running from my worsening eyes, had trickled into my mouth, and I became so parched I feared I should die of thirst. No brickbats at Broadribb: he had spoken unthinkingly and without the least intention of hurting my feelings. What he meant to convey was his amazement that I had lived through the round.

In the eighth I nursed myself with every care, satisfied to ride and dodge this and that punch that would have been a sure winner if any had found the target.

In the ninth and tenth I scored most points. In the next Louis had the better of the exchanges. I won the twelfth, giving many hurtful reminders to Joe that he was in a fight. If I had had two sound eyes and two sound hands I am sure I would have had him groggy. As it was he was obviously worried when he came into the thirteenth. His luck was in. A right-hander that I would have ridden if I had been able to see properly, caught me full on the chin. There was everything in that right-hand, short of murder. It sent red-hot needles into my throat. I feared I would suffocate. I can feel the pain now, after all the years that have gone. Instinct alone saved me. I clinched and hugged until Arthur Donovan separated us. Then, in some miraculous way I recovered normality so far it was possible for a man who had taken such a clout, and to yips and yells and 'Good boy, Tommy', I poked a straight left into the quizzical face of the champion, only, however, to be hit with a trip-hammer of a right full on the forehead. The immediate effect of the blow was to shake me from the crown of my head to my toes. For a second I feared my spine was broken. I did not feel actual pain: I was immune from that by now. For numbed I was. Only my brain functioned.

My eyes were bloody slits, I could just peer through

them and by means of this and that tug at myself, I lasted out the round.

In the fourteenth Louis was again on top, but try as he would he could not land a sleep producer and, I give my word, he tried desperately, frantically. My defence had no holes through which he could send a pile-driver, and I had my good moments, few though they were. I went to my corner to wait a call for the fifteenth and last round, and to cheers that had not died away, with Joby Churchill singing out 'Go in and fight, son', I sought and meant to travel to the end of the round.

Louis came at me at the double. I stood my ground and, having flicked him with a left hand, parried his right. Then a clinch. 'Break,' ordered the referee, and stalking Louis as he backed to the ropes, I held my own at in-fighting. Not only did I make it impossible for him to box in the open, but I could feel that he was being hurt by my short punches.

We finished to a tornado of cheers.

The battle was over, and to my corner I groped: I could scarce see. My mouth was dry and clotted with blood. Yet I was supremely happy. I had gone every inch of the hard, jagged road. I had confounded the critics. I was no pugilistic turtle, no horizontalist, but 'Attaboy, Tommy', so did I hear folks thunder and whoop. 'And,' cried Joby, as he linked my arm to pilot me to my seat, 'Tommy, you've won.'

Words would not come to answer my old and faithful friend. Only tears trickled down my butchered face from a monstrous apology for eyes, that burned and tortured. When I found anchor, long-striding referee Donovan came to take the hand which he raised as I pulled myself upright.

'I've won,' I tried to shout through cut and ghastly

swollen lips, and danced after the way of the wildest der-
vish. I was convulsed with joy . . . but I
misunderstood . . . Arthur Donovan had but lifted my
hand to congratulate me upon 'a wonderful show, Tommy',
and to stir the crowd to further and louder appreciation of
my gallantry.

All the joy, the heat, the ecstasy went out of me. I ran
ice cold . . . I had lost . . . Joe Louis was the winner . . .
and there was Broadribb on the other side of the ring
shaking the gloved hand of the champion.

'Your Joby's here, Tommy,' comforted Churchill, as he
gave me into the care of a transfixed Tom Evans and poker-
faced Jerry Casale. The crowd still cheered and rattled . . .
and stiffening to my full height I threw handshakes. I had
lost and yet won. New York, all America, was my captive.
No beaten fighter could have desired nor could he have
been given a more whole-hearted ovation. I had found the
heart of America. Such were my thoughts and, certainly as
I walked, unaided, to the dressing-room, minding not a
mushed face and eyes from which light was almost completely shut out.

Mike Jacobs was waiting for me with, 'Tahmmy, I'm
mighty proud of you, and that goes for everybody. You've
done what no other guy could have done. You're one of
us. Can you have another crack at Joe? Sure . . . and all
the fights you want. Listen fellah, to the folk out there . . .
they're shouting their mouths off . . . "Tahmmy Farr,
Tahmmy Farr." ' I knew as Mike held and squeezed my
tired hand that in him I had found an all-enduring friend.

Under the pain of damaged eyes and a shockingly pum-
melled face and the treatment applied to my hurts by
Broadribb and my trainer, I fainted. I only came to when

Churchill stuck a lighted cigarette between my lips and called, 'Time's up, Tommy.'

I was taken back to my hotel where, after making a pretence of eating and supping, I was motored to Long Branch.

On the journey to my camp Churchill sang to lie that he was happy: he had taken every thump that Louis sent along: he fought as surely for Tommy Farr and Wales as I had fought, to the last ditch, and he too had taken the full force of the boomerang which the referee unwittingly threw, when after the last blow, he lifted my hand to have us suppose that I had won.

I arrived at my camp to find messages of congratulations without number, and they were still pouring in from everywhere. I was no longer a lone wolf. I was accepted and held to have proved a worthy contender for world honours. Whatever the physical cost I did not grudge . . . and the price was indeed high, as I was painfully reminded when I chanced to look into my bedroom mirror and saw, with eyes which by then were startling peep-holes, that my face was painted in all colours, blue, deep purple, black, green, yellow, and lips cracked and slashed.

I despaired of being again made reasonably presentable. I tried to picture what Louis looked like . . . that he carried an egg-shaped lump under his left eye and that there was a tell-tale puffiness in his brown-black face I already knew, but, said I to myself, 'Tommy, Joe must be an oil-painting compared with your ugly battered mug.' And I had to laugh at the awful caricature of Tommy Farr as shown in the mirror, which in my vanity I ordered Joby to turn to the wall.

There was my broken finger. A doctor was called in and set it, charging £10 good English money, which I decided was pretty stiff. Joby, in white-hot Welsh, declared it to be a barefaced robbery. But he did ever assess values by Tonypandy standards.

I was bucked no end to have read to me out of the morning papers, that I was given unstinted praise for putting up 'a gallant show, and taking the champion to a close decision,' and that 'Tommy Farr gets the big hand'. Dan Parker, the most outspoken of all New York critics, had for his streamer heading, 'FARR WINS MORAL VICTORY'. But referee Donovan's published scorecard gave thirteen rounds to Louis, five to me and found that two were even. Mac Partland's finding was nine to Louis, six to Farr.

I am not disposed to quarrel with Donovan, but . . . Perhaps it is better to leave it at that. I should, however, like to put it on record that in the eighth round, when I had got well into the inside position and was giving Louis furiously to think by the weight I put in blows to his body as he was nailed with his back to the ropes, Donovan did me a disservice by warning me against butting. His caution, for which there was not the slightest justification, recalled the warning given to me by Commissioner Bill Brown at the weigh-in, and his shouted threat that if I did not watch my step I should be fired out of the ring. I got the wind up, so much that I backed into the open and sacrificed a decided advantage. Nothing was more certain than that, if disqualified, I would not be paid a nickel.

I am not suggesting the referee was designedly unfair in that eighth round, but he did me wrong. By ordering me to break, he not only permitted Louis to take a breather, but also to rebuild his defence, in which I had made many gaps.

It is possible that if I had been free to fight my own way,

I would have turned the fight definitely in my favour, my half-seeing eyes and cracked finger notwithstanding.

By what process of reckoning Donovan awarded thirteen rounds to Louis I cannot explain. One critic of international standing wrote on the morning after the fight, 'The verdict is that of a man either blindly partisan or afflicted with astigmatism. It is a verdict that justifies the beliefs that nothing short of the annihilation of Louis would have given Farr victory. That Louis won may not be disputed, but as I read the fight there was only a fractional difference in his favour at the finish.

'The result was hooted loud and long . . . No invader of the American ring within my recollection (and that takes in more years than I care to remember) so emphatically won the good will of the crowd. To his enormous credit Tommy Farr put British boxing on the map, alike by cleverness, courage, self-assurance and honesty of purpose.'

CHAPTER 7

'I guess you're feeling pretty sore,' telephoned Mike Jacobs. 'But get this Tommy, you've saved the ship and I'm going to play you up plenty. I'll be waiting for you at the Garden when you've patched up.'

'Listen Mike,' I squeaked, 'I'm lying low until they've done working on my filleted face. It's a plastic surgeon I'm wanting. No, I'm not coming round for the dough. Freeze on to it until I'm seeable.'

From Pompton Lakes Louis, through his managers, John Roxborough and Julian Black, phoned hearty pats on the back. Within a few hours after the fight stacks of congratulations and messages of good cheer were brought to the Long Branch mansions.

The box-office returns showed that $325,707 had been paid to see the fight. Louis, who was on a percentage, got $102,578. I was on a fixed wage . . . £10,000. My winnings on bets at various odds totted up to round about £3000 and many handsome and valuable presents I received, not a few from strangers. Financially, I was deep in clover, and so too was Joby Churchill, who had gambled all his available cash on my chances.

It required two or three days to take the pulp out of my face. Fomentations, steam, paint, oil, invisible plaster, worked miracles. My eyes however kept the colour of a rainbow and my sight had been so impaired that an optician who was called in ordered the wearing of smoked spectacles.

Horn-rimmed and titivated up, but feeling not a little cheap and self-conscious, I looked up Mike Jacobs at his office. First to collect my cheque and then have Mike open out as to my future in the States.

'Tommy,' he advised, 'better get around before doing business. What's the hurry, anyway? You'll get another shot at the title else you'll be unlucky. But leave everything to me. I've given my word that I'll look after you and what I've said goes. No, I've not booked Max Schmeling for the next Championship. Max has been around waiting to sign. He's never let up asking for Joe since he stopped him before Louis took the title from Jim Braddock, but what he wants and what I'm going to give don't kinda square. He's took on a notion that I'd have him whether I liked it or not.

'I'm telling you again Tommy, that when he signed to fight you in London he was dickering with me. If I had so much as blinked an eye, that "Dutchman" would have been on the first boat out of Hamburg and given you the jump. That's why I sent Sol Strauss to bring you over. Max was using you as a stick to beat me, and I ain't the guy to stand for no funny business.

'Schmeling thought he was the biggest card I could play against Joe, but neither Max nor any goddamn German ain't popular after what Germany has done and is still doing to the Jews. If I had matched Schmeling with Joe and left you out, the fight would have been boycotted, leastways in

New York. The Jews are the best customers and I've got
to string along with them. Max has been here pretty often
this last week or so to ask why he's been frozen out. He
ain't been given no cold shoulder. He wanted to dictate,
and I don't stand for dictators or blackmail.

'You've had one crack at Joe. You deserve another. If
things pan out the way I expect, perhaps before another
year is out, you'll be in the ring with Joe again. But in this
fight business I guess we've all got to wait and see.

'Schmeling has gone back to Germany, where he says he
will keep warmed up until I send for him.

'He'll not come this way until there's no more talk about
boycotting, and then at my own price. And I'm telling you,
Tommy, if and when Max fights Joe, he'll be for it. Max
doesn't know what I know . . . Joe is under an oath to
himself to teach him manners. Maybe you've not heard.
Max looked in at the Lakes to show him the sort of right
hand it was knocked him out a year ago. Joe's a nice quiet
guy, but he can't stand kidding by Max. I ain't no prophet,
Tommy, but I'm figuring that Max will be made already
for the undertaker if he fights Joe. And listen: Max, after
seeing you fight, has gone back mighty glad he didn't swap
punches with you in London.

'You'd have beaten him, not only because you've got
guts, but because your a helluva sight cleverer boxer. And
that's enough for today. Come and stay at my home for a
real heart-to-heart talk, and we'll get out a programme.'

Many happy days I spent at Fairhaven, New Jersey,
where Jacobs lives in grand style. His weekend parties
bespeak the man. They embrace all sorts: there are no
social distinctions, no formalities, no stiff shirts. It's 'come
right in and make yourself at home'. At Fairhaven you see
the real Mike Jacobs, a little old man, 'just tickled' to have

folk around him and for one whole day at least, escape the wear and tear of New York. Never a more expansive man.

'Boys,' he will holler from behind his cocktail bar, 'you don't want to ask for nothing. Just go and get it. No shannanicking. No sidestepping: go to it. Got a thirst? Slake it.'

And the eats . . . No such banquets as at Mike's. No stalling. Guests are expected to take their cue from Mike – feet well under the mahogany table, the more thoroughly to enjoy the feast. No fight talk; not until I sat alone with Mike in his delightful grounds.

'I've had you come here,' he said 'so as to get closer together. I guess you think that one fight is as good as another to me. Most times, yes, but all of them are not alike. Yours was different. Don't tell me. I know. You feared I wouldn't play ball. Kinda suspicious. I'm not for blaming you, Tommy. It's not all up-and-up in this fight game. There's sure no philanthropy. And your Uncle Mike is no philanthropist. I expect and I see that I get a dollar for a dollar, and something over. That's business.

'The guy who doesn't try and kid that he's only thinking about his health is the fellah for me. You've been honest. You've come here to get all the dough you could make, and no secret about it. You trusted nobody until you were sure. Good for you, and in both your ears this: rake in all the dollars you can while the going is good.

'Unless you feel like beating it for home you can stay on my pay roll. You've got a deal to sell, though perhaps not at fancy prices until I arrange for a next fight. Here, there, and round about there's a few hundred dollars to be picked up for a little more than showing yourself – a referee of a ball game, in an exhibition spar – and if you keep clear of the ear biters and tale-pitchers you'll swell your bank roll no end. Always do your walking with both feet on the ground and no harm will get you.

'It's all up to you to prove that you're no sucker.

'First I'll have you shown the sights, and then you'll go to Atlantic City to do exhibitions on the Steel Pier. You'll have Jerry Casale to see you don't bump into no trouble. If there are any rats, Jerry will smell them out.'

The curtain was duly rung up on all the sights of New York, and I was not slow to taste and make feast of the good things.

I was taken around at racing speed, and made dizzy. There were no nights. All days. Sleep snatched at, but never caught. It was a bewildered Tommy Farr who, at the end of the week on the New York merry-go-round, flopped into a car to be motored to Atlantic City with Jerry the Gunman as my minder and a worn out Tom Evans, trainer.

Forty-three thousand people paid a dollar a head to see me spar on the pier at Atlantic City, and of that sum I was guaranteed a generous percentage. Casale collected the money, and he being, if need be, quick on the trigger, was voted the only safe bank. Jerry confided that it was easy to get into the city, but guessed, 'Getting away with the swag might be difficult. I've a kinda hunch we'll be held up. A bagful of grands ain't to be snuffed at by "the boys" who wormed into our party after the show. There's that dame who made herself very pleasant. The guy she's with is no sugar daddy: he's a thug – one of the swell gang. Eyes skinned, Tommy, and don't forget to duck. I'm going to take the wheel going back, which will be after the night show, and when we've had a meal.'

We were all ready for the return journey to New York when the 'dame' of whom Jerry was more than doubtful came to say goodbye. I would not have it that she was other than a perfect lady. And I so far brought Jerry to that way of thinking that he joined in thanking her for telling of this and that road by which we could make New York quicker.

Jerry gave our Cadillac its head. We were in the highest feather until we had burned up some fifty miles, when Jerry, slowing down, called, 'Tommy, there's something screwy. That dame's sure put one over. We ain't making for no places. I always says that dames make suckers of us all, and that goes for Jerry Casale . . . Look.'

Jerry flooded the road with the powerful headlamps and there, a few hundred yards away, was a big car drawn across the middle of the road. Pulling up, Jerry, with his automatic handy, decided to drive straight on and risk a head-on collision.

'We might just scrape through, if we don't find a ditch. The car does not block the whole of the road. So here goes. Sit tight. Under the seat you fellahs and leave the rest to me. If I'm winged that'll be just too bad. It'll be you two guys to fight it out. There ain't going to be no hold-up. My oath on that. I reckon they'll pull in when they see us coming hell for leather. There's yeller in them fellahs in a real show down, and betcha I'm going to call their hand. Now for it . . .'

Throttle full out, the car jumped to a hundred . . . It was a drive to death or safety with all the odds against us. By a whisker we cleared the barricade to scare the wits out of the hi-jacks, and we raced madly to a phone box, at which Jerry, banging on all brakes, stopped.

'This baby,' guessed Casale, 'ain't looking for more trouble . . . a guy can't reckon on luck all the time, and I'm not wanting flowers yet awhile.'

Crossing himself as became a devout Catholic, Jerry rummaged into his stuffed pockets and phoned for the State Troopers to send an escort.

We got back to Long Branch in the early hours of the morning, without further ado. Well to afford laughter at what, to me, was a hair-raising experience.

For the better part of a month I remained the guest of Jacobs. Together with his staff he conspired to give me what he meant to be, and was in fact, the time of my life. His hospitality was overwhelming. I lived in a whirl – lunches, receptions, dinners, night-clubs: and that was how it was.

I was much tempted to make a permanent home in the States. Joby Churchill, however, cabled in Welsh, 'Don't be daft. Come home'. And some five hectic junketing weeks after I fought Louis, I sailed from New York aboard the *Queen Mary*, for Southampton, where I was met by my sisters, who did not require to press me to make straight for Tonypandy, and a family reunion and reception by the townsfolk.

Joby Churchill was all against my going back to New York for anything short of a second fight for the title. 'There's heaps to do in London,' he insisted, 'and quite a lot of money running loose. Accept all the challenges, one after the other, and then go back to America. Besides there's your affairs to settle and straighten out. You're in the bad with the Board of Control, and so far as I can make out they blame you, and will make you pay for calling off the fight with Schmeling.

'It doesn't matter that you have proof that Max would have double-crossed you if Jacobs had matched him with Louis: you have got to make it plain to the Board that rather than being the guilty party, you merely obeyed common sense, which was to see that you were not left without a job, as you would have been if the damned German could have got a shot at the champ. Convince the Board – and that should not be difficult, with all the evidence you have – that Schmeling meant to use you as a tool, and that will be one trouble over and done with. I don't want to go cap in hand, for as I see and know the position, you have done no wrong.'

'Joby,' I answered, 'this is one time that whatever you say will make no difference. I have given my word to Mike Jacobs that my next fight will be for him and I'm not going back on my word.'

'Then,' allowed Joby, 'that's that, but mark my words, you will regret it' . . . And the old man went off in a huff.

Needless to say, differences were quickly smoothed over. A promise to spend Christmas at home helped.

It was planned to be the best and happiest Christmas ever. It was not to be, however. Mike Jacobs, about the second week in December, phoned that he had fixed me to fight Jim Braddock at Madison Square in January, 'and listen Tommy, there's nothing so certain that you'll win. Then you'll be bang in the front line for another shot at Louis. Pack and come straight away.'

I travelled with Tom Evans by road to Southampton, in a Rolls-Royce which, complete with chauffeur, was placed at my disposal by a good London sportsman when I got back from the Louis fight.

We bowled along for the greater part of the journey in silence. Strangely mindful of the sudden vast changes in life as we had known and lived it, I was afraid – lest I woke up and found I was dreaming. By some extraordinary twist I had overnight been taken out of the pit and switched into millionairedom. So it seemed, and scarce could I distinguish between fancies and realities.

'This,' I told myself, 'can't last.'

Try as I would I could not fit in with the new order of things. I imagined folks saying, 'That's Tommy Farr. Coming it strong. Not arf 'e ain't.'

As we drew on to the landing stage I pulled my biggest, heaviest trunk out of the car and, by way of showing I was no 'fresh guy', humped it on to the broad of my back, to the twitterings of porters and shouts from Tom Evans, 'Hey Tommy, what's your game. It's not done to carry your own luggage.' I dropped the package as I would have dropped a hot brick and had it carried with the rest of the baggage onto the *Normandy*, the while I mentally calculated the cost of porterage, and sweated under reminders by a boistrously amused Tom Evans not to forget 'we're posh'.

I tipped with outrageous extravagance, 'just to show that I knew the ropes', but only, I am sure, cutting a ridiculous figure, as I was made into a newsreel by an army of cameramen.

I boarded the *Normandy* at racing speed, but before I could hide in my cabin I was put under arrest by Mr Ben Goetz, head of Metro-Goldwyn-Mayer, who was being 'mighty glad to meet Tommy Farr', and introduced me to Miss Eileen Wenzell, the most beautiful woman, I decided, I had ever seen. Which introduction added to my embarrassment, and I bolted.

'Tommy,' ventured a still laughing Evans, whom I found coatless and collarless in our cabin, 'we've got to do some sprucing up.'

Saying which I set about shedding my fifty shilling suit for a newly bought eight-four shilling rig-out, to the twitterings of my trainer.

A bang on the door, and in walked Victor McLaglen with, 'Hello, big boy; shake. Step out and come and see some of the guys.'

No sooner said than I was being dragooned by McLaglen, breeziest of fellows, into Ben Goetz's suite for presentation to Charles Boyer and his charming wife Pat Patterson, Brian Donlevy, Madeleine Carroll and a host of other cinema stars on their way to spend Christmas at home. And there was in the company the gorgeous Eileen Wenzell. As a rabbit is to a stoat so transfixed I was. There was no escape, and I was glad, so readily was I made to feel that I was not out of joint.

There was no patronage, no high-hatting, I was one of them.

And with the shedding of awkwardness I accepted an invitation to dinner that was the very last word in informality, geniality and the get-together spirit that is the surest leveller of all. I had to tell the story of my fight with Joe Louis in every detail, the physical and moral cost of it. And eloquent tribute did I pay to the mightiness and sportsmanship of the champ.

Morning had come when I was free to rejoin my trainer, whose greeting was that after an early breakfast I was to start daily walks around the deck. Such was my frame of mind that I required no waking up. Sleep was beyond me, and strictly to schedule I set out to do the rounds of the *Normandy* with Evans, intent upon my completing a full dozen circuits.

To my joy Eileen Wenzell joined me in the walk. I was so carried away with her charm and conversation that I took no heed of the number of times I went around the deck, nor the fatigue which my companion must have suffered. Evans, having tired of signalling that I had done more than enough, bawled, 'Tommy, pull in. You have been round twenty-five times. Have a heart for the fair lady.'

I halted just in time to save Eileen from collapsing.

For myself I could have gone tramping to New York for I did walk on air. The truth – I had fallen neck and crop in love.

Transported into hitherto unknown regions I put on a dinner suit for the first time, and was joined by Eileen. After dinner we adjourned to the Starlight Roof, to be again with the kings and queens of the movies.

'Do you dance?' asked Eileen.

For answer I took her in my arms and to intoxicating Strauss waltzed with the rest of the party.

'Tell me,' she asked, 'where did you learn to dance?'

'At Tonypandy four-penny hops,' I replied.

'Some teachers,' she guessed.

'Yes indeed, the best ever. You pay your money, a whole fourpence, takes your choice and there you are, don't you know. That's the way it goes with the boys and girls of Tonypandy. There are no such ballroom dancers.'

'I'll take your word for it Tommy, but do you mind if I say that you have hardly the shape and ways of a guy with a flair for the light fantastic. You are pleasantly surprising.'

Tom Evans crept in to tic-tac his joy.

I called to him in Welsh, 'The Cambrian Colliery is a long way from here.'

'That it is indeed,' he sang, 'and it's Tom Evans that's going to make the ruddy best of it.' And with a merry twinkle in his eye danced with this and the other of the lovelies of the party.

'Tommy, why not distribute your favours impartially,' advised Eileen: and steering me over to Madeleine Carroll, commended me as a desirable partner. Miss Carroll was as gracious as she was an expert dancer – 'some hoofer'.

A night of nights ended all too quickly, though morning had come when the party broke up. And sorry indeed I was when we reached New York.

After paradise and gaiety – loneliness: that was how I felt as I yellow-cabbed with Tom Evans to Essex House, Central Park, where Mike Jacobs had booked me a suite of rooms – seven of them, and three bathrooms.

'Looks as if we are still millionaires, Tommy.'

'What matters most,' I grunted, 'is Eileen Wenzell.'

I sulked myself to sleep until late in the morning after, when the phone rang. It was Eileen calling.

'Would you like to take me out on your first free night?'

'Why certainly,' I red-hotted, and somersaulting out of bed shouted to Evans, 'Tom, it's Eileen. I've got a date, and listen, I don't mind if I spend a fiver!'

'Better be careful,' cautioned Evans. 'A fiver's a fiver, and them gold diggers will be after it.'

'I'll bet you drinks,' I challenged, 'that I'll have lots of change out it.'

'It's a bet,' agreed Evans, 'but don't forget money is counters in New York. There's no razzle to be got out of a five-pound note.'

It was a dandified Tommy Farr, all out for a splash, who went to meet the beautiful Eileen round about eight o'clock. No taxis, no specially hired car. I operated in strict conformity to Tonypandy standards. Like the rare sport she was, Eileen fell in with my ideas of a beano, traipsing here and there, looking in at this swell joint, then another, lying that she had dined before meeting me, content with soft drinks, swearing that a hot-dog and coffee would be fine as a wind-up to a wonderful time, and cordially agreeing that it would be wrong if I overspent.

So we carried on until half-past three in the morning, when I tramped her back to her apartment, where to my sorrow and shame, blistered and butchered feet kept her prisoner for many days.

'Tommy,' she phoned as she rested, 'next time out you might cut out the hobo stuff. Once is enough, but I understand. You could not help being Tommy Farr, and I'm glad that you were your own natural self and not a fresh guy. Oh yes, you are forgiven, but between now and next time I'll be sure that foot-slogging is an acquired taste, certainly not recommended by my chiropodist, nor must it be favoured by Tommy Farr when he again takes on the role of Sir Galahad.'

Truly I had asked for and was given a lesson in chivalry.

Yet in my incurable frugal-mindedness I counted the winning of the bet with trainer Evans a notable triumph. . . . My first night out with gorgeous Eileen Wenzell left me with £3 15s out of the fiver I was prepared to squander if put to it.

CHAPTER 8

Off I went next morning to Madame Bey's training camp to get down to work for Braddock, and when I came to figure things out I was convinced that Jim must be pretty well washed up.

Still, I was taking no chances. I worked like a beaver from the day I went into camp and my shape so pleased the critics that long odds on my winning were offered. And there were few takers.

It is to me a familiar and painful history that Braddock was returned the winner on points at the end of ten rounds. When his hand was raised by the referee I was flabbergasted, and so too was every impartial critic.

In round after round I out-boxed and out-fought 'the old man.' There were moments when Joe Gould, his manager, was about to give up the ghost. When Braddock realized that he had been given the decision he was no less surprised than I was. Except for courage, Jim won no marks. I'm giving away no secrets . . . It is a fact that when the last round was called, Gould told Braddock that his only chance was to knock me out. Said I to Tom Evans, 'This is where there's going to be no mistake. Tom, I'm a sure winner. He's all in and I'm good enough for another ten rounds.'

This is what happened. Braddock, who had the Irish element with him to a man (how they rooted for him), came to me like a dancing doll, for all the world as if he were shadow-boxing, like a looking-glass fighter as we say, and to the gallery it must have seemed that he had not only taken on a new lease of fighting life, but with his whirling gloves was scoring all the points.

At any rate they cheered him to an echo. Actually Braddock was under instructions to caper so as to disguise leg weariness. He buzzed around like a mosquito, but he could neither sting nor hurt. He could do no more than flick: he was without a punch of serious account. None the less he had the crowd with him.

If I had had the least doubt that he could catch up to me I would have let go all I had, but I was so far in the lead that he would have had to force me to take the count to win. All I had to do was wait for the bell. There was not the least reason why I should make a toe-to-toe fight of it in the last three minutes. I could not imagine the referee being swayed by the crowd, so I held to a defence which Braddock had utterly failed to break down. When the last bell clanged I said to myself, 'That puts paid to Jim Braddock.'

To say that I was amazed when it was bawled 'Braddock's the winner', would be to put it charitably. I was so staggered that I might have been hit by a thunderbolt.

Braddock came over to my corner with Jim Gould to shake hands. I was so beside myself that I had no stomach for niceties.

'Hard luck, Tommy,' commiserated Jim.

I shot daggers of looks and made haste to the dressing-room to cool off. My show of temper was wrong of course, but I challenge each and everyone of the thousands who saw the fight to reconcile the verdict with bare justice. If I had not beaten Jim Braddock I had never won a fight in my life. Responsible newspaper critics lampooned the referee for giving a 'sentimental victory' to the 'old man', and in words that permitted of no mistake, declared that he was all wrong in his reading of the fight.

For my part I was sure I had been given a particularly raw deal and equally certain that Braddock to his dying day would be baffled to know how he got first home.

Mike Jacobs had a deal to say that was not for publication. It would ill become me to put it on record. Enough that he was sore and was with me entirely.

'Mike,' I swore, 'after this I'm through with America. You can have no use for me now. No squealing, but since it has gone on record that I lost the Braddock fight what earthly chance have I got for another title fight? None.'

'Listen,' commanded Mike, 'you're sure shooting nonsense. I'm not saying you've not had a bad deal and I'm doing no stroking of you down. But I'm telling you – I've been in this fight racket and all sorts of rackets long enough to know that a guy who curses his luck don't get nowhere, no how. The referee says you lost – you're not going to get him to say you won. The job of the fighters is to do the fighting. A referee decides right or wrong: he's the law. Maybe he's not on the level, maybe he's not got the courage of his convictions, but what can fighters do? They've no kick. They must grin and abide. Tough maybe, but fighting's tough whether done in or out of the ring.

'That leastways is life as I know and have lived it. I've lost count of the times I've won and yet lost. I reckon it'll always be the same until I've played the last hand. That's what the high-hatters call philosophy, and if you're a wise guy you'll take on a load of it. It'll help you to forgive and forget. But get this: you're not quitting America, and I'm not going to throw you over. Neither are folk here. "The sentimental victory of Jim Braddock" will soon be forgotten.

'You see, Tommy, Jim was underdog, and human nature is quick to react to the guy who brings off a long shot. Take it from your Uncle Mike that if you had put one over Joe Louis the shouts would have been for Tommy Farr. All the clever guys who are now saying that there's never been a champ like Joe would have writ that they knew Joe was full of holes, just because a "certainty" had come unstuck.

'Champions are made to unmake . . . It was thought when Braddock was pulled out for you, he was finished. I thought so too. He surprised everybody, himself most of all. I want you for Joe: I'm not too hot on Max Schmeling: it's up to you. True you've had two fights here and lost both, but your stock stands just as high as it did after you took Joe all the way.

'We've got all the world champions, but I'm thinking that if a Britisher took a hold of the heavyweight title it would be all to the good of the game. Mind, I don't think there's a big fellow to beat Joe, but if the opposition is not big enough to pull the best out of him there's bound to be a slump. I've never been on your side of the Atlantic and can't say what's wrong. But it cannot be that the old country has stopped breeding real fighters. The head and front of boxing would be changed for the better if we could look to and depend upon Britain to produce fighters at every weight against the best in America. I've been around a long while, but I am all for international fights, same as was the great Tex Rickard. Tex had a vision. Who but far-seeing Tex would have brought Carpentier over and put him against Jack Dempsey? They said he was crazy, but he got all the laughs. He conjured 100,000 people to the fight. $1,789,238 into the locker, of which Dempsey got $300,000 and Carpentier $200,000. Maybe Tex scooped the pool, but I'm telling you there are more million-dollar gates to be had if and when our champions go to war with real live colourful contenders from overseas.'

'Mike,' I broke in, 'I'm staying.'

'Good for you,' said Mike, 'and,' he went on, 'your next fight will be with Max Baer. Beat him and – well, we'll see. He'll not be easy: leastways they're telling me he's never been in such wonderful shape.'

I fell into the scheme of things with no question or quibble and at once cabled Churchill. Joby's reply was, 'Don't. There's all the fighting you want at home and money too. You're still daft.'

I decided that for once I knew better than Joby. Events proved that he was dead right. That, however, is another story.

Having given myself over to Jacobs lock, stock and barrel and so booked for an indefinite stay in the States, I put myself under the management of Joe Gould. That meant parting company with Ted Broadribb, and to my sorrow, the making of many troubles and misunderstandings for which, when I got back to London, I paid a considerable amount in hard cash. The change-over cost me thousands of pounds. When I settled all claims there was little left over from what I got for the fight with Louis. No complaints on that score, however.

I paid the price and nothing more need be said.

Joe Gould has the reputation of being, and is in fact,

110

one of the shrewdest managers in the world. It was Gould who took Jim Braddock out of the breadline and made him champion.

In every regard he served me well. I did not know, when we joined up, that he had had a deal to do in paving the way for my fight with Baer.

'Tommy,' he confided, 'this a-way I figured. Jim Braddock is through: he's had his fling. I'm mighty pleased he finished on a winning note, though at your expense. Me and Jim have been fingers crossed from the first day he began fighting. And what he (and that goes for me) went through to get into big dough no one knows. He deserved all that's come his way.'

'But Joe,' I asked, 'do you honestly believe that Jim did beat me?'

He drawled, 'Forget it and let's get busy with Maxie.'

'OK,' I agreed, 'but Joe, you'll let me have a grouse, won't you.'

'What's the good?' he inquired. 'The big idea is Maxie. I'm gambling good and plenty that you'll put the skids on him, and get right back in line for Joe. If I did not think that you'll be back in the ring with the champ before another year has gone, Joe Gould would not have asked to take you over.'

I interrupted, 'Given a fair deal, I'm sure as a man can be that I shall beat Max Baer again. He's done no fighting since he stopped Ben Ford in London and that's nearly a year ago. Such a long lay-off is not in his favour. At least he can hardly be as good as he was at Harringay.'

'Tommy,' warned Joe, 'Maxie has wakened up. He's different. Dead serious. No more gallivanting for the big boy. The clown that was in Maxie is dead. Ancil Hoffman tolled the bell. Forget that Maxie has been out of the ring all this while. He's never left off working since he came back from Europe. That's why I'm all for you fighting him. He's your big chance to get another shot at Louis. Beat him and you'll forget that Jim Braddock ever lived.'

The fight with Baer was two months after the Braddock bombshell. All went well with my training, though now and then I was plagued by my eyes, which were not so clear-seeing as they might have been. A feeling of immense bodily strength and limitless stamina, however, dispelled what fear I had that my eyes had been permanently impaired by the injuries I suffered in the battle with Louis.

I ducked under the ropes at Madison Square Garden on the night of 11 March 1938, brimful of confidence.

With Max was mountainous Buddy. Ancil Hoffman, of course, and Jerry the Gunman, my old bodyguard. It seemed strange to see Jerry in the opposition corner, but there he was, an avowed champion of Max.

'Tahmmy,' Max declared as he grabbed my hand, 'this is going to be a fight and then some.'

'Indeed it is, Max,' I assured him. 'Another Harringay, eh?'

'Yep,' he laughed, 'but I guess the boot'll be on the other foot this time.'

And grinning, he went over to babble with his corner.

'The same old Max,' I whispered to Gould, 'all bubble and squeak. A great guy.'

'Oh yep,' drawled Gould, 'but he ain't the same. He's out for blood, and listen, there'll be no fooling.'

Joe Gould was right. Max came out fighting, his eyes afire. Feinting with his left hand he let go his right, but he was out of distance and I jabbed him on the nose.

'Good for you,' he twitted, and bang with all his might he drove left and right into my ribs. And how he hurt. I

112

feared something had snapped. It was a poor pretence of a smile I made as I held my ground. To my surprise Max fell on the defensive, and weaving in I punched him with both hands to the body. The end of the round came at a moment when we were giving blow for blow, to the shouted joy of the gallery.

'Tommy,' advised Gould, 'go out and fight with all you have. Max wants it that way. Let him have it. You've got as much as he has. Maybe a little more. He can't travel as fast as you can, and see, he's worrying about his puffing eye. Don't say he'll quit, but you'll slow him up if you keep close and bang away at his stomach. That's your target Tommy, his middle.'

I made complete surrender to Joe's advice and was encouraged no end to find that without a deal of finessing, I could force myself into the inside position and bring purple patches round about the ribs of Max. But hammer as I would, Max could not be bent. Except for an occasional grunt as I rammed home this and that fist, his only real trouble, apparently, was a fast-blackening patch under his eye. In clinches he gave me the sharpest reminders of his abnormal strength, and always was I pleased when 'Break' was ordered, for then, almost invariably, I scored with my left hand. I was a shade in front at the finish of the second round. And to Gould, as I sat in my corner, I said 'If I can box, I can win.'

'Tommy, you can outfight him. Fight while you're strong,' commanded Joe.

I followed instructions. Perhaps, I decided, Joe knows best. And, besides, I had promised to do as I was told. I tabled everything. Also did Max. We went at it belt tinker. I never punched harder, nor did Max, I swear.

I thought my number had gone up when Louis dynamited my jaw at the Yankee Stadium, and again when he crashed a right to my forehead, but though those two punches were near to the death of me, they were no more terrible than a couple of swings I took from Max, each of which floored me, in the fifth round.

After each punch Baer stepped back expecting to find me all stretched out. Then (I know not how, for I was cruelly hurt) I pinked him on the nose, and in obedience to instinct went into a clinch, to shouts of 'Finish him, Max' from Hoffman.

We had gone a trifle more than half the distance (the fight called for fifteen rounds) when Baer showed signs of tiredness. We had asked and given no quarter, and according to my mental calculations I was a good head in front of what had been a gruelling race from the first bell. His body had taken on the colour of liver. His eye was then coal black, and almost closed.

I confess that I too was much under the weather, but outwardly at any rate, not nearly in such bad shape. On my legs I was as firm as a rock, and signalled no distress to my corner, as did Max.

'Maxie's cracking,' said Gould, as he worked furiously at the end of the eighth round. I made no answer, for though I had seen Baer wobble, I could not bring myself to believe that he would buckle up.

I remembered that he had sworn to avenge his defeat at Harringay, that for nearly a year he had been in regular training, that he was not only fighting for Max Baer, but Mrs Baer and baby Baer, and above all, to make good his word that he had done with clowning.

'Joe,' I said to Gould, 'Max will only be through when he's down and out to the world.'

I was right. Baer changed from an apprehensive to a

114

murderous Baer, but I was blind to the transformation. Instead of boxing as I surely should have done, I took a leaf out of his book. I preferred out-and-out fighting.

After what had happened in the Braddock affair, I was convinced that only by fighting with the lid off would I find the way to victory. Overboard went caution, and in the fourteenth round Baer brought his pole-axe to my swaying, weaving head and then smashed it into the pit of my stomach. Ever come a cropper on the ice when skating: ever taken the other fellow's boot in the belly when playing football? Well, that was how I felt when Baer sunk his right into my stomach in that fourteenth round. Screams to 'Kill him' came from every part of the Garden. By a superhuman effort I pumped breath into my contorted body and though Baer made a barrage of all the best in him, I lasted until the bell.

Sick near to death I was as my seconds worked on me until the call for the last round. How futile it seemed to be told, as I was again by Gould, to 'Go in and fight him, Tahmmy.'

Pretty nearly all that was left in me was an iron determination to last the distance. 'Fight him, Tahmmy.' What mockery. For in sore need of mending were my bellows. The more tantalizing was the orderliness of my mind. There I was, a fighter with but a little disturbed mentality, so burgled of wind that the most I could do was to deny Baer a knockout. Believe me, Max tried all he knew to apply the closure.

I refused to be knocked for six, and to my tremendously pleasant surprise, was feeling immeasurably better and stronger generally when I set out for the last round. Max won all right, and I was the first to congratulate him on his victory and the perfect fairness of his fighting.

'Tommy,' he said, 'it might've gone your way. You're a great guy. You made me know I was in a fight all right. You've left me with only one peeper. Guess I'll not be around for some days. How are you feeling? Pretty sore I reckon. So is Maxie. They told me you couldn't punch. How they lied. It's Maxie Baer who knows, not the guys who look on.'

That I was cast down goes without saying, but full marks to Baer: never had he reached a higher standard of skill. It must have been that he fooled away the title when he fought Jim Braddock.

I did not require to be told in words and print that I met a better-than-ever Max Baer. He was a great fighter on that March night at Madison Square, and a rare sportsman.

Three fights in New York: three defeats. So it went on record.

'Joe,' I said to Gould, 'I don't know how you feel about it. Pretty rotten, eh? What about a showdown?'

'I know what you're thinking,' he answered. 'You reckon that in taking you over, I made a bad deal, kinda bought a pig in a poke. That's not Joe Gould. I'm carrying on and Tommy Farr is going with me all the way. No turning back. I bought your contract to make money, and we'll pay dividends. It's a sure thing that you're not going to buy yourself back. What kind of fighter is the guy who can't take the rough with the smooth? A palooka. The boys used to say "here comes Joe Gould with that Braddock fellah." They would not have given a nickle for him. I was bats, they said, and if Jim had had the last word, he would have kicked it in. The big-shots wouldn't look at him, but I held on and, well, didn't he take the title from Maxie Baer, with any odds against him?

'But you are different. You are young, have a nice bank

116

roll, and you're a helluva sight more popular than when you happened here. Step out of yourself and leave the rest to me. I'll do the talking. You'll do the fighting when I've got out a programme, which as I figure will not be yet awhile. There's got to be no getting rich quick. No need to hurry at all. I have Mike Jacobs's word that you are still high up on his list, and that's more than good enough for me.'

I did not dare tell Gould that at that very moment I had a cable from Joby Churchill stuffed in my pocket, begging me to come home and straighten up my affairs that threatened to get into a hopeless tangle. I hadn't the heart, nor would any other fighter in my state of mind and condition have opened out.

It was with all my tongue in my cheek that I agreed that he knew best.

And Gould, basking in the hot sun of super-optimism, prescribed, much to my delight, a long holiday. And as will a conjurer produce a rabbit out of his hat Joe produced a couple of tickets for Hollywood, and a bunch of introductions to 'all the swell guys'.

In less time than it takes to tell I was flying with the adorable Eileen Wenzell to Chicago, en route to California. Walter Winchell, the famous columnist (was there ever such a lynx-eyed, all-ears fellow?) paragraphed the trip, and by way of adding spice, enlarged upon 'Tommy Farr's crush'.

'Eileen,' I said, 'this Winchell guy knows something. What about it . . . Let's . . .' We became engaged. It was roses all the way to Hollywood where, though the hour was early a platoon of reporters and cameramen were waiting to reduce us to news and pictures.

To think and talk coherently was impossible, as I was

grabbed and interviewed and generally turned upside down and made out to be this and that which I was not.

It was a terrifically hot-collared young man that escorted Eileen to our hotel, where under the sobering influence of a desperately needed shower, I silently calculated the cost of the trip in good hard cash. With a boiling-over temperature I realized the impossibility of escape.

'But there is Eileen and nothing else matters,' I comforted myself. And smacking my lips in contemplation of the wondrous time, I took on a boldness that surprised even myself.

Diffidence gave way to enchantment. From then on I had no time for rumination. Hollywood and forgetfulness mean one and the same thing. I was unspeakably happy; and yet at odd moments I was shy to believe that I had come to a real flesh and blood world. So it was that, after our first evening meal, I suspected a conspiracy to pull my leg when I lifted the telephone to hear a voice asking 'Is that Tommy Farr? This is Clark Gable.'

To which I made the answer. 'If that's Clark Gable this is Norma Shearer.'

'Whose wanting you, Tommy?' inquired Eileen.

'Someone trying to kid me he's Clark Gable,' I replied.

'Don't hang up, whoever it might be. Why shouldn't it be Clark Gable?' pouted Eileen.

Well, it *was* the one and only Clark Gable, offering 'Welcome to Hollywood, and congrats on your wonderful fight with Joe Louis. I couldn't make the Yankee Stadium, but bet your life I drank it all in as it came over the radio.'

I met Gable at the studio later, and found him to be free, frank and human, no ostentation, no distinctions. In some subtle yet unquestionable way I was made to feel that I belonged to Hollywood. It was all contrary to what I expected. Big, expansive, without the least littleness. All my pre-conceived notions were exploded.

Clark Gable is typical of the 'stars', an immense worker with the priceless gift of making friends.

If there be an idea that movie stars go through their days junketing, let it be killed stone dead.

CHAPTER 9

First impressions of Hollywood may suggest an unexampled playground; actually it is a hive of industry ever buzzing. It is not the capital of frivol and frolic. None the less, the blare and dazzle of it leaves the stranger blinking, intoxicated.

Hollywood has a heart, all embracing. Maybe I was especially favoured. In truth I was. From my first meeting with Clark Gable I was accepted and adopted.

I met everybody who counted and away from the studios, at work and at play . . . George Raft, Pat O'Brien, James Cagney, Victor McLaglen, Humphrey Bogart, Mae West, Leo Carillo, Tony Martin, Errol Flynn, Edward G. Robinson, Dorothy Lamour, Joan Crawford, Alice Faye, Carol Lombard, Betty Grable, Barbara Stanwyck, Eleanor Powell . . . all the stars.

Bing Crosby had me dine with him at his house. A more delightful host could not be found. His knowledge of boxing and boxers is intimate and profound.

'Tommy,' he broke in on ringside experiences, 'I've yet to meet a good Welshman who could not sing. What about it? Some of your folk songs, eh?'

'After you,' I begged.

'It's your turn first.'

There was no denying Bing. From nowhere, so it seemed, he produced his accompanist, and I led off with an old Welsh hymn and, at his request, *Land of My Fathers*.

'And that,' I said, 'is all.'

'Tommy,' he smiled, 'that was grand.' Of course I knew he was only kidding me.

Thereupon Bing sang as only he can sing. I would not be content until he had sung at least half a dozen numbers.

I saw much of him during a five weeks stay in Hollywood, and he was always the same – precisely himself, an artist to the finger tips, a rare sportsman.

On one of my many visits to the studios, I was taken to see Shirley Temple [probably the best-known film star of the 1930s. She was now aged 10], from whom I'd had a message: 'You must not forget to come round. I shall be waiting for you.' A most remarkable little lady. Precocious, no. Clever, intelligent, astonishingly so; but absolutely unspoiled.

'Mr Farr,' she led off, 'when I've got through, we'll have ever such a long talk. I've been promised that I can stay up after my bedtime, and you must tell me all about your fight with Joe Louis.'

'But,' I excused, 'what is there to say?'

'Lots,' she decided. 'You don't mind, do you? I'm frightfully interested. You see, I heard the story over the radio, but now you are here I want the *real* story. It will be ever so much better than the broadcast.'

'It's a long story, and perhaps you'll tire,' I warned.

'Oh dear no, I'll not fall asleep, so there.'

And when we were alone I scarce knew how to begin.

121

She came to the rescue by giving me her version of what happened.

'I'm afraid,' she suggested, 'I got it all wrong. It's for you to put me wise.'

She would have no sketchiness. I had to take her through the fight round by round. When by way of finishing I said, 'And now it's time to ring down the curtain,' she loosened a barrage of questions, to make sure that no detail had escaped her.

'Mr Farr,' she said, 'I can now say that I have seen the fight. I shall never forget. Louis must have been wonderful, as you say he was. But you too were wonderful. You've made me sorry that you lost.'

'That,' I reminded her, 'is how the game of fighting goes. There has to be a winner and a loser.'

'But,' she encouraged, as she gave herself over to her mother, 'next time, perhaps, it will be different. I hope so.'

When, with Eileen, I was not with the stars in their homes, I was exploring every nook and corner of Hollywood. Now the dream houses in Beverly Hills, again the studios. Wednesday night is the 'maid's night out' and homes are closed down. Then it is at the Trocadero Restaurant that one may see and make feast of life and gaiety.

I made a point of arriving early on Wednesdays at the Trocadero and saw to it that I had a table as near to the entrance as possible, to watch the comings and goings. For hours I would sit spellbound, toying with food, taking wine foreign to my plebian palate, and in ever re-occurring Tonypandy moments, fearing that I would not outrun the constable. The panorama, the splendour, the unusualness of it, however, was more than value for money; I was taken out of my severely provincial self and enraptured.

THUS FARR

A cable from Joe Gould calling me to New York brought me up with a jolt. But I was not allowed to steal away, as I was much tempted to do. George Raft and Pat O'Brien entertained me to a farewell dinner at Coconut Grove, Los Angeles. Of a distinguished party there was James Cagney, Errol Flynn, Victor McLaglen, Humphrey Bogart, Bing Crosby, Tony Martin, Dorothy Lamour and many other highlights. That dinner will ever remain an ineffaceable memory that I devoutly hope will be possible to revive in the happier days to come.

The morning after the Raft-O'Brien farewell dinner I drove to Burbank Airport, with Eileen. It was a feeble attempt that I made at cheeriness, and she for her part was painfully subdued.

Boarding the plane, I was taken out of a brown study by a lady passenger who asked, 'And are you the famous Tommy Farr? I'm Luise Rainer. How do you do? You go to New York. So do I. It's a long journey and it would be nice to get acquainted.'

I found speech, of which the parting from Eileen had robbed me, and never could 3600 miles journey have passed more quickly.

Brilliant, witty, fascinating Luise. I needed many tugs at myself to make sure that I was flying with Luise Rainer, whose performance in *The Good Earth* I had seen but a few days before. Then she seemed so far away, so unreal and yet real. Now she was my immediate companion on a voyage through the air, regaling me with her experiences, her ideas, and views on, and attitude to everyday life.

'I've yet to see my first prize-fight,' she confessed. 'And here I am with a real live prize-fighter. But I forget that you are Tommy Farr, the fighter. I see in you an entertainer with all the differences. You write and play your own

123

script. You owe no obedience to directors. Is that not so? What you call your own boss, a freelance. It is up to you to produce results: if you don't it is finis. That is a gamble, life as it will ever be, and as I would have it. When I went to Hollywood they would have had me tied to long contracts. That I feared would steal my own self. I refused to be chained for an indefinite period. I preferred work into which I could put my everything at three hundred dollars a week, to a sky-high salary.'

Capricious Luise Rainer. Not only did she crave for, but insisted upon, freedom of action and thought. 'Perhaps there is a rebel in me. But no matter. I am happy with my work and my public . . . and for you. If you are not booked, will you come along with me to the opening night of Clifford Odets' new play *The Golden Boy*? He as you must know, is my husband, and *Golden Boy* is what you call in your street the romance, the joys, the tragedy of a prize-fighter.'

We came down to Newark (New Jersey) to be met by the usual newspaper men and photographers. James Roosevelt, son of the President, who had joined the plane at Kansas City, stood by while I was snapped with Miss Rainer.

'Won't you come into the line of fire, Mr Roosevelt?' invited the cameramen.

'Oh no,' he excused, 'I'm not for spoiling the picture, but you can shoot me with Tommy Farr.'

'OK,' chorused the photographers, and with a promise which, need I say I kept, to escort Luise Rainer to the theatre that evening, I drove away with Joe Gould.

With characteristic tact Gould waited until the following day before tabling his plans. Then I learned that he had booked me to fight Lou Nova for Mike Jacobs at the Garden.

'But I say Tommy, what's got you?' he asked. 'You look all washed up.'

There was nothing for it but to confess that I was feeling worse than cheap. My eyes plagued. My chest wheezed all the tunes. A doctor was promptly called in. He put me to bed, where I was kept for a couple of weeks.

To ensure what was hoped would be a complete cure, I was sent to Commissioner Bill Brown's health farm at Garrison on the Hudson, a delightful place. No coddling, up at 4.30; 5 o'clock physical jerks, cold shower and massage; breakfast at seven; hiking from 8 o'clock to 11, followed by oxodised treatment. Lunch at 12.30. A rest, then horse riding across country. An early evening meal, something of a banquet, 8.30 bed, lights out. Spartan life with a vengeance, but it spared me a physical and nervous collapse.

I left the health farm with Joe Gould for Doc Beir's training camp at Pompton Lakes to start training for Nova. Doc Beir, a noted physical culturist, having run the rule over me, strongly advised me not to think of fighting for months.

'But,' I stamped, 'I've given my word to fight Nova, and there's going to be no backing out. I'm committed to obligations I'm bound to meet.'

'It's your funeral, Tommy,' he warned.

'Listen Doc,' I protested, 'you are not going to talk me onto the shelf. I've seen Nova and I'll lick him for sure, even if I'm only half fit. What do you say, Joe?'

'It's up to you, Tommy,' said Gould.

I cut the cackle and started light training which I spread over little longer than a week. I had no sooner got down to serious work, however, than I was laid low with a sharp attack of bronchitis. I was quickly nursed back to what was decided was reasonable shape, and with the approval of my manager I resumed work. I much missed the sea breezes of Long Branch, and bitingly cold weather put a heavy premium on road work. Still, with Gould, I hugged to a certainty that I would stop Nova inside the distance.

As luck would have it, a blizzard raged on the night of the fight. Few people ventured to the Garden, and being on a percentage all I got for my end was $610 for the fight, which was a fifteen-rounder.

From the opening to the last bell I did the attacking.

Nova was all for boxing by numbers at the dictation of his corner. 'Make him mix it,' Gould dinned at the end of each round.

Nova was having none. Safety first was his watchword, and oftener than not when I was in a fair way of nailing him close, it was my bad luck to be ordered to break. Then Nova would waltz around, content to flick and flap and make such a pretence with his long left, which he stuck out straight and kept rigid.

His style, if style it could be called, had no more than the virtue of awkwardness, and according to my own and Gould's reckoning, I was always comfortably in front.

'Tommy,' snapped Gould at mid-distance, 'you've got to knock this baby out. Keep on fighting and you'll break him into little pieces.'

Now, Nova did not look tough, but he was, and dead game. Otherwise he would have crumpled under the showers of body blows I rained upon him. Often I could feel him wince, but he somehow kept up. All the betting was that he would not go to the finish. But he did, and got the verdict.

'Joe,' I said to Gould, 'perhaps you'll tell me on an off day, how the scoring is done here.'

'Don't ask me,' he begged, 'it's just too bad.'

'It is, and worse,' I bawled. 'Don't tell me it'll be different next time. There can be no next time after this. I'm not saying that I beat Joe Louis, nor Baer, but I did beat Braddock and I've just beaten Nova, and nothing will convince me that I didn't.

Confessed Joe, 'I haven't the language to say what I want to say. But what'd be the good anyway. It's up to us to show 'em and that can only be done by fighting.'

'But who next?' I inquired, with I'm sorry to say, not a little show of temper.

'I'll be seeing you,' promised Joe after letting off his own steam.

Less than a week later Gould, upon whose advice I kept in light training, asked, 'What about Red Burman?'

'Why not?' I replied. And Burman, at one time Jack Dempsey's chauffeur, who had not lost one of his last eleven fights, it was.

We were put on in mid-January following my December fight with Nova, at the Garden. I made it a condition that no matter what the result, there must be a return match in London.

How pleased I was that I made that stipulation, for according to the official scorecard (which I swear was outrageously wrong) Red beat me on points. Into the details of the fight, however, I beg for special reasons to be excused. For everybody's concern it was best forgotten.

'Joe,' I cursed, 'it's not enough that I'm terribly sick, but short of slaughtering the other fellow I'll never be the winner. I'm beating it home by the next boat. I'm through.'

'Pipe down Tommy,' advised Joe, 'you're overdue for an overhaul by the doctors.'

At the earliest opportunity I sailed home, if not a sadder, a vastly wiser young man – to find that Len Harvey, having beaten Eddie Phillips on a foul, had been crowned by the Board of Control. Protestations that fights were decided in the ring, not in the boardroom were of no avail. I had not only been dethroned, but by way of rubbing it in the Board ordered me to pay a fine of £750 for not fighting Schmeling, without first checking their apparent theory that I had wilfully and designedly run away from the German.

To the part of an injured innocent I have never aspired, but I am free to maintain that it would have been more in keeping with everyday fairness if the custodians of British boxing had asked for an explanation why I did not go on with the match with Schmeling. In condemning me, they condemned Mike Jacobs on purely circumstantial evidence that could have been disproved by documentary evidence. I have no desire to re-open old sores, and I am not without hope of being acquitted from the wrong that was charged against me by the Government of my native ring. I paid the fine, and made full settlement with Ted Broadribb for whatever loss he suffered when I broke with him and put myself under the management of Joe Gould.

Red Burman followed me to London roughly a month after he was given the decision at the Garden. With him came Maxie Waxman and Harry Jeffra, otherwise Ignacius Pasqualia Guiffi, who had won and lost the world feather-weight title against Joey Archibald.

Waxman, it will perhaps be remembered, brought Vince Dundee, then the credited best middleweight, for a return match with Len Harvey, who twice lost to him in New York. Harvey, almost at the last moment, was unable to take the ring owing to illness and Jack Hood, at the shortest notice, stepped in to make a draw with the famous American.

What Maxie Waxman does not know about men and things isn't worth knowing. The rough and the smooth – it's all the same to him. Morning, noon and night he's always to be found on the premises. If he ever sleeps it is with one eye open. A man to have on your side, decidedly. Dempsey puts much store in Maxie, who is as big as he's plausible. Only the American ring could beget the likes of Maxie. He's a man for any job, the soul of adaptability, a profound student of psychology. So it was that Burman, whose front name by the way is Clarence, could not have been in better hands. Jeffra was specially engaged to speed him up. He served his purpose admirably, as to be expected, for Jeffra, at his poundage, was a remarkably clever boxer and an expert trainer.

Sydney Hulls promoted the fight and put it on at Harringay and, as he deserved, made a nice profit for himself. As was natural, I was, to say the least, curious to see how my countrymen would react to my American experiences. It was encouraging to have news from promoter Hulls that as a box-office proposition the fight was a winner.

And yet I was not entirely happy in my training.

'One mistake,' I told myself, 'and it will be your finish.'

For all I worked and sweated in the gym, my confidence seemed to have left me. Nothing was the same as in preparation for fights with Ford, Baer and Neusel. It was like beginning all over again. It needed the understanding, the sympathy of Joby Churchill and the arrival of Joe Gould to get me to see things in the right perspective.

When I got into the ring the crowd brought me back to complete normality by their full throated ovation. Much did I owe to those thousands of cheering folk. Ever shall I be their debtor. Their rousing welcome home changed me from an over-wrought Tommy Farr to a self-contained Tommy Farr with no misgiving whatever.

Joe Gould, in Britain for the first time, who was in my corner, whispered, 'Tommy, now I understand your people. They said they were ice cold: they are red hot. I'm mighty glad I made the trip to see for myself. They're swell.'

I said, 'Now you have the answer why I itched to come home.'

Burman, as he came over to shake hands, was breeziness itself, and trained to the minute. As I went into action, I said to myself, 'This is where I'm going to box and fight my own way, and make certain of winning.'

Burman, under orders to unloosen all he had immediately, let go a vicious right. I ducked clear and jabbed him on the nose. Before he had time to sniff, I was banging away at his body without, however, doing serious damage. A brush I took on the chin decided me to try to out-box him before attempting to thump to victory. There was little in it in the first round. I should say that it was level pegging, but from then on I took the full measure of Burman, piling up points and landing the more telling blows. At half distance, if not before, I had Burman so bewildered that whenever I shot out my left, I found his Irish face and made generous play with the right. More than once under clips to the jaw he was dazed and looked like going down and staying down.

Only an extraordinary capacity for taking punishment and the running assurances of Maxie Waxman that he had a winning punch, kept him going. I could hear Chewing-Gum Maxie rasp at the end of each round as he sponged the cut and bruised face of Burman, 'Red, you've only to swing one over and the fight's yours.'

Red would shake his carroty top as if to answer 'Sure, Maxie, I'll get him next time.'

So it went until the twelfth round, Burman always the receiver-general. And then I was returned the winner.

It was allowed that no other verdict was possible. Not even a mild kick came from Burman or any of his party. He made many friends during his stay and would have come back but for the war. I have an idea that he was paid more money by Hulls than he received in any of his previous fights. He was abundantly satisfied with his end and so, I am sure, was Maxie Waxman, and Maxie was never cheap.

Waxman 'collected' shortly after breakfast on the morning after the fight and off he rushed, with Joe Gould leading the way, for Southampton to catch the boat about to sail for New York.

Gould's farewell was, 'Don't forget, Tommy, I'll be waiting on the other side with all the fights you want and bags of dough.'

I had already decided to remain at home for a year at least during which time I might be given an opportunity to prove that despite the Board of Control's ruling, I ranked first among British and Empire heavyweights. Sydney Hulls, at my urging request, threw out feelers to Len Harvey, who a month before I turned the tables on Burman, had knocked out Larry Gains at Harringay in the thirteenth round. At the same time, I tabled an omnibus challenge.

In the matter of Harvey I drew a blank. I don't suggest that Len was dead against fighting me, but his terms, together with the price I considered I was worth as the undefeated champion, were such that there was nothing doing. If I remember aright, Harvey wanted something in the neighbourhood of £7000, but even if I had taken a couple of thousand less than that amount, the total cost was more than any promoter would pay. Hulls calculated that to satisfy Harvey and myself, he would have to find anything up to £12,000 with little chance of making any wages himself.

It would perhaps ill become me to say that it was a pity that Harvey did stake his title against me. He might retort that since I was sure that I could beat him, I should have been content to accept a much lower figure than he wanted.

On the principle that every man is free to put a price on his own head, Harvey was quite right in holding out for his terms, but with every deference I will have it that except by the kind permission of the Board, he was not entitled to an appreciably bigger fee than I was prepared to accept. But perhaps if we had known that war was so near, we would have assessed our respective values less high and settled to the satisfaction of a considerable public a much debated question – whether Len Harvey was the more entitled to wear the heavyweight crown than undefeated champion Tommy Farr.

I was encouraged to suppose that if I fought and made shorter work of Larry Gains than Harvey had done a few weeks before my fight with Burman, the Board of Control would at least nominate me No 2 heavyweight and so pave the way to a match with Len. With that idea I agreed with Hulls to go to Cardiff for Larry.

Gains, for his part, broadcast from his training quarters that he was all keyed up, and a deal of capital was made of the fact that last time out he had gone thirteen rounds with Harvey. Also was it recalled that before fighting Len, he defeated George James, who was being touted as a sure champion of the near future.

I had not fought in Wales for the better part of three years, not since I won the Welsh heavyweight championship by knocking out Jim Wilde at Swansea. Longer than that since my last appearance in Cardiff when I was paid less than training expenses. The fight caught on from the day articles were signed. About it there is little to say except that after keeping Gains on the defensive from the start, I stopped him in the fifth round.

The fight was so one sided that not a few of the critics who had enlarged upon the wonderful shape of Gains and his many qualities, thought it a pity that the match was made. Little or no credit was given to me for doing immeasurably better than Harvey had done against the former Empire champion.

The very purpose of the fight so far as I and a discriminating public were concerned, was to stop Gains in less time that it took Harvey short of two months previously and thus establish an indisputable right to a title fight with Len. In the position I was put by the Board, it was the logical thing to do. If the Board had had the least doubt of the worthiness of Gains, they should have barred the match. It was with their full approval that I fought Gains, and I cannot recollect any responsible critic objecting to the contest on the score of inequality. But no matter the post-mortemists. I had no cause to reproach myself. The contrary – I went away from Cardiff considerably the richer in pocket and with high hopes that weight of public opinion would force a fight between Harvey and myself.

Cables and repeated telephone calls from Joe Gould and Mike Jacobs to return to New York I ignored. I determined that I would not go back to the States until I had again proved beyond all question that I was champion heavyweight of Great Britain and the Empire.

'Harvey or nothing,' that was my battle cry. So as to be on the spot I settled in London, but Harvey preferred to fight Jock McAvoy for the cruiser title. Two months later came the war and straightaway I enlisted in the Royal Air Force.

CHAPTER 10

Before joining up I had contracted to fight Manuel Abrew, the coloured Scottish heavyweight, whom I had knocked out four years previously in the sixth round at the White City. The return match was to be at the Theatre Royal, Dublin, two months after the outbreak of war. Given leave of absence, I flew to Ireland a few days before I was due in the ring.

I was met at the Dublin Airport and played to my hotel by the Hibernian Pipe Band. To my dismay, on reaching the hotel, I was handed a bundle of letters by the porter, threatening death if I went on with the fight. Two, as from 'The Irish Republican Army Headquarters,' and signed 'Few but Fearless', were especially disturbing. 'If', I read, 'you are after good Irish money, it's a dead man you'll be.'

I was disposed to treat the letters as a joke until I was requested to meet 'two young ladies who are waiting for you in the lounge,' and told by them that unless I handed over £100 to the Party Fund, there would be trouble.

'Stop your kidding,' I laughed. 'What's the Party Fund anyway? What do you take me for? A piecan? Beat it little girls, and pronto.'

135

'You are going to drop or be dropped,' hissed the spokeswoman.

'Well now,' I sidestepped, 'if it's like that I'll be a phil-anthropist for once in my life. Come around tomorrow and I'll cough up like the sucker you take me for. But first what about one for the road to drink to the success of the "Party Fund".' Whereupon, with tilted noses the 'depu-tation' took themselves off.

As they went through the swing doors I made a beeline for the telephone and told the police what had happened. Also I contacted the promoter of the fight. The outcome was that I was put under the protection of a couple of detectives. I professed amusement. Actually, I carried an uncomfortable feeling in the pit of the stomach. Positively, I was scared.

Even when the college boys bid me welcome and placed their gymnasium at my disposal, I found it impossible to capture peace of mind. For stuffed in my pocket were further and ominous reminders of the 'Party Fund'. Never-theless I held to my notorious tight-fistedness and took whatever the chances of 'sudden death'.

I was smuggled out of the hotel perhaps an hour before the fight was due, and escorted by devious ways to the theatre which as a precautionary measure I entered by an unsuspected back door. I got into fighting clobber at once and was giving a perfect imitation of a hen on hot bricks when a knock at the door and 'Ready, Tommy Farr?'

White about the gills, with hair on end, I walked into the auditorium and climbed under the ropes. The theatre was packed. Five days before, every seat had been sold.

I waved my hand by way of greeting the crowd. Dead silence, not a whisper of a cheer. I shivered and with head down slunk to my corner with legs as heavy as lead and a wind-up severely vertical. When I was called to the centre of the ring by the referee for 'instructions', however, I was cheered to the echo. It was a tonic I had prayed for. The gentleman in charge thought it necessary to interpret the rules and give the usual cautions through a megaphone and was so long winded and pompous as to set up wholesale fidgeting.

I said to myself as I went into action, 'This is no occasion for cleverness. It's got to be the trip-hammer or nothing.'

I walked straight up to Abrew and before he had time to build any sort of defence, hooked him with a vicious left and crossed him with the right. Down he went. I thought it was all over. Instead, he only took a short count and as I went in to finish it with all caution overboard, he slung a right from the neighbourhood of his ankles and clipped me on the jaw to hurt a lot. A breather, and then crowding on all sail I hammered with all I had. Again he went down, but clutching the ropes managed to pull himself up and last out the round. I rushed into the second round and stopped him racing around with a swinging right that landed full into his stomach, and forcing him on the ropes I uppercut him with a right. Once again he dropped and again he brought himself into the perpendicular with the aid of the ropes.

I straightened him out with a left-hander that went plonk on to his generous nose and the while he blinked I ripped a right to his liver that sent him rolling on the floor and out to the wide world.

I did not wait for the verdict. I made for the dressing-room at the double and was back in my hotel long before the theatre had emptied, with my detective escort at my elbow.

As I made for my room a note was handed me. It read,

'Leave the £100 at the desk for collection. If you don't you'll not get out of Dublin alive.' For a signature, skull and crossbones.

Feverishly did I wait for daybreak when I was driven to the airport and away I flew to Liverpool an hour before scheduled time for my departure. 'And that,' I decided as I landed on Merseyside, 'is the last fight I will have in Dublin.'

My experiences in Dublin were as a holiday in Arcadia compared to what befell me after reporting for duty. My health broke down completely and I was discharged as being totally unfit for service in any branch of His Majesty's armed forces. I returned to civil life a physical wreck with, I was warned, little hope of regaining normality. Partial blindness threatened, lung trouble developed, injuries I had suffered in the ring seriously affected my hearing and I was lighter by a couple of stone (30 lbs).

For days and nights and weeks I stormed and raved and cried hysterically and so locked myself in a dungeon of hopelessness and despair.

'There is no future,' I cursed. But there was pumped into me a philosophy common to the sick and weary that broke my fall over the precipice. And the good, understanding Joby Churchill came to help in my salvation with burning words of wisdom.

'Tommy,' he soothed, 'there may be only a shell of your old self left, but it will not crack into little pieces unless you so will it. With your money you can have the finest doctors and the best of nursing. It will be a long, heartbreaking job, no doubt, but it can be done and then you may tell, chapter and verse, why you are not in the services. The world can be and often is unkind. The cry went up so soon as you were invalided out of the Air Force.

"Tommy Farr has swung the lead all right". And take my word for it, you'll be hearing worse than that before you are much older.'

How right Joby was. But despite quizzical noses, innuendoes and vilification, I was not prepared for the question asked by Mr Evelyn Walkden in the House of Commons, 'Why was Tommy Farr, the prize-fighter, not in the forces?' Whether Mr Walkden was carried away by his own verbosity I may only guess. But without the least mincing of words he would have it that I had bluffed my way back to civilian life and held me up to scorn for being a shirker.

As a protest against his outburst of righteous indignation I wrote to him as follows:

Mr Walkden,

I have just returned from doing a series of shows for the troops and in my mail I had quite a number of clippings sent to me with your remarks concerning me in the House.

To say that I am flattered at having my name mentioned in the House is putting it mildly, but you yourself, Mr Walkden, should be rather ashamed of yourself, don't you think, to slander my name from your safe and secure seat.

We British always pride ourselves in giving everyone a square deal. You possibly are an exception to our treasured tradition.

Everything I hold dear in this world depends on this life and death struggle we are now in, so how can you have the audacity to say 'Is it bluff.' For you to question my sincerity makes me ill, but then your daily associations might have given you a one-track mind. If you are interested, I will furnish proof of my four applications to join the fighting forces and also the Medical Board's certificates of my troubles.

You will also please note that I never wish to risk my life or defend my country in a cushy PT Instructor's job, shouting and bawling all day . . . something that you seem pretty useful in doing . . . but as an air-gunner did I enlist three days after the declaration of war and on three other occasions I tried unsuccessfully to join the actual fighting forces.

I might have thought you would have had a little more to do, seeing the very heavy responsibilities you MPs must be bearing these days, not to wilfully slander my name. As an MP I should have thought that you of all people would have attempted to find out the truth before committing such a flagrant slander.

Anyway, possibly we will meet some day.

By way of clearing up misapprehensions and in common fairness, this is the true story of what happened from the day I enlisted until I was discharged as totally unfit, my long battle against illness and repeated efforts to get accepted by one or other of the services.

Three days after the outbreak of war, I went from London, where I was living, to Cardiff recruiting depot for enlistment in the RAF. Doctors who examined me were doubtful of my eyes, but whether because of my assurances that there was nothing radically wrong or my razor-edged keenness, whatever my physical defects, I was accepted and proceeded to the reception unit where I was met by a PT Officer whose welcome was a hearty pat on the back and 'Good boy Tommy. You are doing a good thing for the youth and morale of the country.' Which cordial greeting bucked me up no end. 'The human touch,' I decided.

I was immediately sent to a smallish town in Lancashire to be assigned. All the fellows there were delighted to see

me and I was put full on my toes. Sent back to Cardiff, I
went to the PT Officer in a belief and certainty that in him
I had found a pal. I knocked at the door of his office and
walked in. Instead of taking my proffered hand he glared
as he bawled, 'Tommy Farr, where's your kit?'

'What do you mean by kit?' I asked.

'You know what I mean, man,' he snapped.

Before I could untie my tongue he roared, 'Farr, you are
now in His Majesty's forces and from now on you take
your orders from me. You just don't knock at the door
and walk in. You knock and wait until you are called in.
You stand at attention, salute and call me Sir.'

I was dumfounded and spluttering, 'I thought you were
my friend, all out to help and put me to the rights generally.' I locked the door of his office and took my coat off.
I was mad with passion and meant to give him the thrashing
of his life.

Mercifully, the red that had shot into my eyes gave way
to straight thinking. I reached for and put on my coat,
unlocked the door, jumped to attention, saluted and with
all humility begged his pardon.

'That's all right, Farr,' he laughed. 'I only meant to see
what you were made of.'

'My mistake,' I readily confessed. 'I thought you were
taking a rise out of me and I hate to be made a chump.'

'Forget it,' he rasped. 'You'll learn . . . the quicker the
better, or else.'

I was sent for by the Commanding Officer. 'Farr,' he
said, 'I'm glad you have not waited to be called up. I am
proud that you have not only not shirked your duty, but
forgotten that during the past few years you have enjoyed
much success and met and been entertained by, shall I say,

all the best people. You might have fallen to the temptation to hang back, or at least tried for a softer job.'

From then on I appreciated to the full the difference between an officer and a gentleman and a commissioned barker and bully.

For the second time I was ordered to Lancashire. A finer bunch of fellows could not have been, though I am bound to confess that upon first acquaintance they wanted a lot of understanding. Their dialect was beyond me entirely, their sense of humour as pawky as it was profound.

Huts that served as billets were not rainproof, not by a long chalk. But that was a detail which I freely allowed to 'Titch', a little queer-shaped fellow who, taking me under his wing, prepared me for 'muck and nettles.' 'And,' he went on by way of further marking my card, 'if tha gets that stuck in thi craw, tha'll be aw reight. Nowt has got to matter in this ruddy show. Seen t'corporal yet? No. Well that will in t'morning and tha'll not forget him in a hurry.'

'Thanks a lot, Titch,' and with that I joined the rest for a much wanted night's sleep. My luck was dead out. My trestled bed was not meant for a six-footer, neither were the blankets which when pulled up left my generous feet all exposed and set the hut rocking with laughter.

'I'll tell thee what,' advised my next-bed neighbour, 'ger up and tuck t'clothes in at t'foot. Then try sliding down under them. Th'll find tha feet'll get warm if nowt else. Go on and have a do.'

To the 'blimey, take a decko at King Kong' of a perky Cockney, I tried the experimental dive, but it wouldn't work and half covered and doubled up I chased sleep that refused to be caught, which with one accord, was voted to be as good as a pantomime.

With peep-holes for eyes, feeling like nothing on earth,

we were barked up by the corporal at 5.45 a.m., dressed under drippings from the roof and blinking, listened to, 'Now then, you lads, get yourselves shaved and spruced.'

His command obeyed, we were lined up for inspection. Thoroughgoing, the corporal went from the top to the bottom of the line stroking each chin. He had to tip-toe to reach my jaw, which he OKd but with this reservation: 'Next time you shave, stand a few yards closer to the razor.'

Breakfast plonked on our plates soon over, I paraded with the other recruits before the corporal for a 'pep talk'.

'Now then, you fellows,' he began, 'this is your first day in the Air Force and I reckon that all of you want to get somewhere. That you can only do if you remember that I'm the governor round here. You do what I tell you and at the quick, see.'

'Yes, sir,' we chimed with one voice.

Inwardly chortling, I suspected, the corporal called me over for 'just a few words'.

'You are Tommy Farr, the fighter, aren't you?' he asked. 'Well, don't forget we tame lions here.'

With a 'Yes, corporal,' I left him to preen and strut and bark.

If ever a man made revel of his vices and hid his virtues it was that Corporal. There was a heap of goodness in him, though to say the least his methods were decidedly quaint, at times uproariously funny. A bull terrier made up as a whippet.

I fell for him neck and crop. Off the record, so to say, he was a real chum. So too was my sergeant; on occasions, the three of us came to London together on leave.

Once I got the hang of things, everything promised well. The day when I would have qualified as an air-gunner seemed pleasantly near when on a perishingly cold and rainy morning at PT drill, something snapped inside me and blood trickled from my mouth. I was put to bed for a couple of days and given a thorough overhauling by the Medical Officer and other doctors. The upshot was that I was recommended for and given my discharge.

My forced farewell to all the good and big-hearted boys at the air station hurt me as hard as the findings of the doctors. It meant the tearing of myself from the happiest of families. I felt that I had let my team down.

'But,' I promised them, 'I'll be back.'

Truth was I wanted to howl.

'Scrapped, useless Tommy Farr,' I fell to muttering on the long, and so it seemed, unending journey from Lancashire to London. What a finish. Hamstrung out to the world. Rich in pocket, but in health poorer than a beggar.

There followed a round of treatment by specialists, nursing-homes and hospitals. First I was operated on for throat and ear trouble. That done, I was put under the care of a famous optician who feared that I would lose the sight of my right eye.

I left for Brighton and for an agonizing week I was kept in a darkened room. If I had not cried incessantly, I would have gone mad. 'Tommy Farr's blind,' I imagined it being whispered.

Mr William Lloyd, the optician, came to visit me and advised me to give myself over to a Mr Reeves of Wimpole Street in London. He said, 'If there is one man who can save your sight, it is Mr Reeves.'

It was found that the optic nerve had been burned by, probably, some particularly stringent lotion that at some time or other had been used to stop bleeding from eyes cut in a fight. Happily, my sight was so far mended that although it could not be brought back to normal, it was saved.

Against the improvement in my sight, I suffered acutely from lung trouble and scared I was at my loss of weight. I became lighter by 17 lbs and down the hill I kept going.

However, the best medical treatment procurable, careful nursing and Brighton air worked wonders, and off I went to Cardiff to see Captain Geoffrey Crawshay, Chief Commissioner for Wales, with high hopes that since I had known him personally, I might get into a Welsh regiment. The army doctors, however, also refused me. 'You would be a liability and a danger,' they said.

Back once again to London to moon and mope. I asked myself, 'Why not try for mine-sweeping? That's the ticket.' And away I went to Yarmouth.

'Just the type of fellow we want,' I was voted. But it was inquired, 'What sea service have you had?'

I told them that I had crossed the Atlantic eight times.

'In the *Queen Mary*, the *Normandy* and the like, eh,' it was laughed. 'That's not good enough. Much as we would like to have you, you'll not do. You must have had two years sea service.'

Determined to have another shot, I went to the recruiting office at Wembley. 'Your name?' I was asked.

'Thomas George Farr,' I answered.

'Occupation?'

'Miner.' I had the idea that as such I would have a better chance of being taken in. Again I was condemned.

Following a medical examination came a declaration of my physical unfitness. I was given no grade, not even a C3. So back to a wilderness of despair. Worse, once again my health broke down. The root trouble this time had to do with throat, nose and ears.

There was nothing for it, I decided, but a foremost Harley Street specialist. An operation was advised and performed at the Ewell and Epsom hospital where, plugged and tubed, I remained for some time. During my stay there London had its worst blitz and bombs fell hair-raisingly close to the hospital.

As I lay propped up, I could see London's sky ablaze and it was as if the roar of planes overhead would never cease. The sisters, nurses and staff generally were wonderful. How glorious their make-believe that 'It's nothing.' How high and challenging their heads. Steel nerved, they shut out any danger of panic, thundering defiance at the murderers of the skies; and in her soft trippings here and there, my Welsh nurse would sing-song to my helpless, silently swearing self, 'We can take it, Tommy, can't we. It's nothing.' I choked with admiration for that Welsh woman and the angels who tiptoed to and fro without batting an eye, though death was all around.

I decided that as soon as I was untubed I would take French leave. When the matron came into my room and found me fully dressed, making a desperate attempt to smoke a cigarette, she ordered me back to bed with, 'How dare you.'

'Matron,' I pleaded, 'I've simply got to go home. You have been and are all so kind, but you've got your hands more than full without me, and well . . . I'm going, and nothing will stop me.'

She gave way to my stubbornness, but only after a tremendous fight, and I drove down to my Brighton home.

A reoccurrence of the throat and nose trouble developed, and after consultation with a Brighton specialist, I had a diseased bone removed from the back of my nose. Another legacy of the ring. It was a long and delicate operation and yet within a quarter of an hour after being wheeled away, I was caught smoking a cigarette, to the horror of the nurse. How the puffs of that smoke hurt, but it was worth all the maddening pain.

For months after returning home I was slow to recover, but rest, rigid diet and nursing so far brought me round and gave me back the weight I had lost that I built myself a gymnasium and by light and judicious training, found that I was physically competent to give exhibition spars by way of entertaining the troops.

I have given shows at widely different centres – Dundee, up in Scotland, to the furthest corner of Wales, with special regard for places far off the beaten track, unmindful of weather conditions, and whatever the cost to health or pocket.

Everyone, of all ages, was obsessed with 'doing their bit' towards the war effort. My 'bit' was little enough, but with the doors of each of the services closed to me, it was all that a sick and turned down Tommy Farr could give.

It was during the months that I was climbing from this sorrowful state that I met the woman who was to change my life, Muriel Montgomery Germon. A beautiful red-head who agreed to marry me. And in 1940 she bore me a daughter, the first of three children. Two more sons forthcoming.

I have had more than a few ups and downs over the years, culminating in my making what the critics called my 'comeback'. But there were bills to pay and kids to educate and feed, and the tax-man was on my tail.

The rest is history and is irrelevant to that which I have just told, simply because my life changed so utterly after marriage.

THUS FARR

I am as happy as a man in his right mind. I owe everything to boxing and boxing does not owe me a thing.

THE LAST PHASE
by
GARY FARR

'I am as happy as a man in his right mind.'

How true he was. To the end he maintained a lucid and humble humour that captivated all who met him.

He was a very sick man as he concludes his story and it was to take months of convalescence before he would be back to normal. For whatever reason, he never got round to finishing the story; maybe – and this is what I suspect – he simply considered it a closed book. It was certainly true that after he left the ring a series of business enterprises went sour and he was left to struggle very hard to provide for his family, so if nothing else his time was cut out.

His family meant a very great deal to him. When he came back from America in 1939 he had been secretly married for a year to Carol Montgomery. That was her stage name. Her real name was Muriel Montgomery Germon. She was born in British Columbia, Canada, and was a couple of years younger than my father, something of a bombshell in the burgeoning British film and fashion world, making a good living modelling for advertisements. They met, fell in love and married, and kept it secret for nearly three years.

Within a year of marriage she presented Tommy with Rosalind Ann. Two years later came Thomas Richard and two years after that me, Gary Anthony.

Although my father cuts short on any more talk about Eileen Wenzell, his American sweetheart, my mother tells me, with no rancour whatsoever, that he went back to America twice before settling down. The relationship between the red-headed Monty, as he called her, and my father was an obvious love match; they were to be together for very nearly fifty years and were hardly ever separated throughout that time. Monty was a law unto herself, quickly established herself as both best friend and wife, and was very popular with their crowd.

When Tommy left the ring in the very early days of the war, he had some money but not enough to last for ever. An opportunity arose, however, and he bought a pub in Brighton, a booming coastal town some fifty miles due south of London where the family had settled in a huge old manor house called Glovers on the Upper Drive.

The pub was called the Royal Standard and was a stone's throw away from the railway station. Next door to it he opened a restaurant called Tommy Farr's Pantry, and both establishments enjoyed great popularity for five or six years under the management of his brothers John and Doug.

Unfortunately the fame of the owner attracted a certain bunch of clientele who, as they became drunker, identified the more with the fight photographs that adorned the walls. Late one night John phoned him at home and advised him to come quick. Once there he found Doug on his back being badly beaten by a French Canadian seaman. Tommy sorted the situation out with little trouble: a slap here, a slap there.

Next day the headline was, 'Tommy Farr Involved in

Street Brawl'. It went to court, and Tommy lost his publican's licence.

Within a year he was involved in a book-making business that lead him into flirting with Lady Luck and got him in pretty deep with the racing crowd. He bought several horses, backed them heavily, lost heavily until he was cleaned out completely. He blew an estimated £25,000, a fortune in those days.

However, he had invested in some prime property on the sea front in Hove, a town adjoining Brighton. It was something to fall back on – until the government introduced a property tax which put him into complete penury.

He sold the big house Glovers and bought a smaller one in Wilbury Road, Hove. There, in near despair one evening, he asked Monty, 'What can I do? All I'm good at it seems is boxing, using my bloody fists.'

My mother said, 'Then box, man – if that's what you want.' It was not what she wanted, but still she said it. Next morning he was not in the bed when she awoke. He was out running, beginning the training to start the long climb back. This was in late 1950, and he was 37 years of age.

He was in the ring once again on 21 March 1951. In the next ten months he fought seven times, winning five of the bouts, including regaining the Welsh heavyweight title. All his opponents were much younger than he, but he was on the way back, and making money to pay off the debts that had piled up. Monty looked after the paperwork. No manager this time: more money for them.

His last fight was in 1953, just before his fortieth birthday, against the great hope of the day Don Cockell, who was only in his early twenties. The fight was stopped in the seventh round.

My father, still rather scornful of Cockell's abilities, nevertheless admitted, 'If someone like him can put me down, it's time to quit.'

So his career finally ended on a low note. But in this second phase he had done what he intended: pay the tax man, settle his gambling debts and ensure his three children an education.

Once more, though, he was virtually up against the wall. Then, on a brainwave, he rang a friend of his, George Casey, who was sports editor of the big-circulation national newspaper the *Sunday Pictorial*. The result was a job writing a weekly boxing column at a quite handsome salary. For twenty years he did that, until the *Pictorial* became the *Sunday Mirror* and there was no room for him.

Another slim period, broke and getting broker. They moved first to a much smaller house (we kids had by now left home) in Goldstone Crescent, Hove, and finally to a bungalow on the beach at Shoreham, a not too lovely spot just along the coast.

By then he was representing a company that specialized in industrial paint. For sixteen years he did that, drawing upon the respect afforded him by his contempories and upon his own inherent intelligence. The Admiralty, oil companies, ship yards – you name it, where paint was painted my father hustled.

Eventually he visited California to spend a Christmas with me and my brother, then went back to Shoreham. There he died peacefully a few weeks later, in February 1986.

My brother and I were able to visit him the week before he went. For that I will always be glad. He was very, very sick, knew that he was on the way out, but his dignity was massive. Once he knew that his boys would take care of laying his body to rest and – most important – of the looking after of his beloved Monty, he gave up the struggle. He went in his sleep, in his bed, in the house with his mate. A few days later my mother was shifting the furniture in the room and found a sheet of paper under his bed; on it she read the words of the last poem he wrote her, fallen where it had slipped from his weakening grasp.

It was not until I began editing *Thus Farr* that I realized that my father, infallible to me when I was a child, had screwed up his career.

If he had not got sucked into America and committed himself to Mike Jacobs . . . if he had not made the Hollywood trip with Eileen . . . the cigarettes, the booze, late nights hanging around the stars. It doesn't take much to lose your edge in the ring.

All the time out there he was encouraged by those who had his career in their hands to go out and 'have a good time'. You have to ask the question: why?

And the decisions on the fights in America. The key one was almost certainly the Louis fight, a moral victory for my father if not a technical one. I think it was this that earned him the Yankee rancour that made for the travesties of boxing justice in his subsequent battles on American soil.

But all the time he was tasting too deeply of the good things of life there was no one around to remind him of his foolishness. No Joby Churchill. No Ted Broadribb to goad him into greater efforts. He'd been on his own. Totally unprepared for the smoothies of New York.

History knows the truth, but my father, the sportsman to the end, would never have complained at the way he was treated by the boxing moguls of New York. As I look at it he would have been more than justified at griping. But not a word of it.

I wonder, though, what would have been if he had come back to Britain after the Louis fight, waited for the Yanks to come to him, stayed away from the fleshpots and kept in prime condition?

Undeniably he would have entrenched himself as the only British and European heavyweight; probably fought and beaten Schmeling; had another shot at Louis and maybe have won, become world champion.

Who knows?

Among his papers was one other essay, a short one, written I suppose in 1950 or 1951, telling why he was making his comeback. It seems apt to close this book with it – fitting, too, to give him the last word.

WHY I AM
COMING BACK
by
TOMMY FARR

For many months I have fought an urge to come back with a challenge to the world's heavyweights.

I have lost.

The urge is unconquerable. From this very day, fighting is again my business. The shutters are down; the shop wide open. I stand at the ready, behind the counter, hoping, itching, for worthwhile customers – Savold, Comiskey, Bechor – any top-ranking American for choice.

I have no objections to trading punches with any Britisher, but my first ambition is to avenge their defeat by Americans, and if Joe Louis is seriously disposed to come back, as is probable, he may be certain that I would be delighted to have his patronage. I court the strongest opposition.

'Tommy Farr,' I can hear it chorused, 'is impossibly vain or in sore need of brain-scraping if he supposes he will be taken at his own valuation.'

None the less, I would have it believed that I am wholly sincere and that I am not eaten up with immodesty, and that if I were not convinced of the rediscovery of the best that was ever in me I would not have the brazenness, the stupidity, to invite the British boxing public, to whom I owe so much, to share my certainty that there is no rustiness in either my mental or physical make-up.

I do solemnly declare that I have not, in any vital particular, worsened since, with pardonable joy, I killed stone dead the idea that a British heavyweight was another name for a horizontalist.

I hung up my gloves to settle down to married life and a normal everyday job, and I prospered (I found every happiness in domesticity). Children, three of them, came to make for a merry-go-round I had but dreamed of. Within recent times, the dice of life which, since retirement from the ring, had run consistently and long in my favour, became loaded against me – a matter upon which for the moment I will not enlarge.

The last straw was a fragrant announcement for everybody to see and read, that Tommy Farr was broke – to the unbounded joy of the knockers.

Tommy Farr is not broke, I am glad to say, not even bent or dented. Bulging, bottomless pockets he may not have, but destitution, no. Emphatically no.

That agreed, together with my assurance that I am not on the rocks, I ask it to be believed that it is not so much wanted money that has decided me to make again my trade in the ring, where I was tossed when but a boy, born to fight against all the odds for his bread and butter.

I make no pretences – a well is never too full of fresh water that it would be bettered for a trickle. I do swear, however, that if I may be permitted to make good my word that, despite a long lay-off, I am without a kink, I shall be abundantly satisfied, for then I will well and truly have served British boxing.

Whatever may be said of the extravagances, the vanities,

the ups and downs, or the eccentricities if you will, of Tommy Farr, you cannot say that he did not have the courage of his convictions. It is nine months ago that I fell to wondering whether, if I applied myself to intensive training, I could get so close to fighting completion as to silence the lampooners of our big fellows.

I took the view, shared by all non-partisan appraisers and valuers, that with the standing down of Joe Louis, the rest of the American heavyweight brigade were not invincible. Holding my own counsel tight, I thus put myself through a searching analysis, with the fixed idea that if by diligent, wholehearted training, I ironed out this and that soft spot, I would, in the event of Bruce Woodcock losing to Lee Savold, step off the shelf.

I rooted for Bruce, none the more furiously, and by way of encouragement credited him with qualities which, after I had had him on my dissecting table, I found him to be without. But I would say that Lady Luck didn't always smile on him kindly.

Even so, I could not see in Savold the invincible world-beater, so I went back to my home with my mind made up. Said I to myself, 'Given the opportunity, I will avenge Bruce.'

Early that next morning I was again pounding around the grounds, all unknown except to myself, as I had made a habit of doing for some months previously. And then back to my gymnasium for shadow-boxing and such ground exercises that I went through in preparation for my Louis fight.

Strangely enough, with being a few years older, the exercising and gymnasium routine seemed easier and not so much of a grind as it used to be. I have been helped and heartened immeasurably by the fact that I have never allowed myself to run to seed – the children see to that. To say I am four pounds lighter than when I fought Joe Louis, speaks for my condition.

No pulling the longbow, we British have been modest long enough. I take my oath that I am fitter today than when I fought for the heavyweight championship of the world.

I am stronger and my hands are stone-hard, something I did not enjoy in those earlier days, and my speed is equal to what it was in 1937. I have been expertly timed and have not been slower than eleven and a half seconds over 100 yards for the past six months. I am punching very hard and my timing has satisfied me. In years I am still gloriously young. I refuse to be dated and could not be richer in experience.

This is why I am coming back to the ring.

I trust the experts will not judge me until I have had an opportunity to prove my words.

I fear no boomerang. I am coming back confident that my refound fighting self will give a fillip to British boxing, remembering, of course, that I should hate my kids' school pals to tell them that their father 'just didn't make the grade'.